D0425389

LOVE THE ONE YOU LOVE

825 CARING GESTURES

Beth Kitzinger and
Linda Davies Rockey

FOREWORD BY
TAMARA TRAEDER

This book was originally published as
Creative Caring.

MJF BOOKS
NEW YORK

Published by MJF Books
Fine Communications
Two Lincoln Square
60 West 66th Street
New York, NY 10023

Love the One You Love
Library of Congress Catalog Card Number 99-70068
ISBN 1-56731-325-6

Copyright © 1997 by Linda Davies Rockey and Elizabeth Kitzinger

This edition published by arrangement with Wildcat Canyon Press, a division of Circulus Publishing Group, Inc.

This book was originally published as *Creative Caring: 825 Little Gestures That Mean a Lot.*

Interior Design: Gordon Chun Design
Typesetting: Holly A. Taines

All rights reserved. No part of this publication may be reproduced or transmitted in any form or by any means, electronic or mechanical, including photocopy, recording, or any information storage and retrieval system, without the prior written permission of the publisher.

Manufactured in the United States of America on acid-free paper

MJF Books and the MJF colophon are trademarks of Fine Creative Media, Inc.

10   9   8   7   6   5   4   3   2   1

Contents

Acknowledgments

We would like to gratefully acknowledge the many people who have shared their personal stories with us for this book.

We also wish to thank our many friends and family who supported us through this project. You helped us to pursue our dream, often just through encouraging words. We give special thanks to our children, Allison, Chad, and Jay, for trying to understand our passion and commitment to this book.

Kudos to everyone at Wildcat Canyon Press for believing in us. A special thank you to Roy M. Carlisle who kept us inspired during the process of creating this book. And to Holly A. Taines for her special editorial contributions to the final text.

We have to acknowledge the friendship that we share as co-authors. As best friends for twenty years, completing this book together has expanded our friendship. The book would not have been possible without each other's support.

Mostly, we appreciate the kindnesses that have been shown to us as we have traveled the path of life. Any sign of compassion enriches our life and gives us renewed hope for the future. To be cared for, supported, and encouraged are as essential to our well being as water and food. Our lives have been made richer by being able to care for others. The act of showing kindness to others is the greatest gift we can give ourselves.

Caring in an Uncaring World

As we look at the world around us, it seems to be an uncaring place. Bombarded by media images of starvation, homelessness, and poverty, we often are left wondering "What can I do?" Even on a smaller scale, the number of problems and challenges faced by the people in our immediate circle of family, friends, and community members sometimes seem too numerous to address. Most of us have experienced the feeling that every one of our friends or family members is going through a crisis simultaneously. We often feel powerless, or awkward and ineffective, when we face the unending need for compassion and care that loved ones require. What can we as individuals do?

The answer is that we do what we can in the world that we know. While we may contribute money or goods to organizations that help others in the rest of the world, one-on-one caring, like charity, begins at home. And home means our circle, the circle of people we care about and interact with on a regular basis. So what stops us when we see a need? We may feel reluctant to interfere or invade the privacy of others. Or we might fear doing the wrong thing, failing to answer the need of the person we are trying to help.

We may hesitate at the prospect of helping others, especially those outside our immediate family circle. Others' misfortunes may bring up negative feelings about ourselves and our lives that we may not want to face. Additionally, when faced with an illness, crisis, or family problem of someone we do not know that well, we often worry that our offers of help will make them feel uncomfortable: "They will be embarrassed or self-conscious if they know I am aware of their problem, so I'll pretend I don't know." In a small town a veil of secrecy may cover a person's illness or family problem; what is meant as politeness may also cloak the problems of someone we know only in a professional capacity. Unfortunately, our silence may be interpreted as disapproval or indifference, and the person in need can be left feeling isolated and lonely.

We simply may not know what to say or do. If we feel awkward and unsure of ourselves, we oftentimes don't do anything. In the past, we might have jumped in and made a supportive gesture that turned out not to be appropriate. We might have come away from that experience feeling like a bull in a china shop, vaguely realizing that our action was not helpful to the person in need. Our intentions may be good, but when left to guess how best to help someone we may have guessed *wrong*.

Caring can be a complicated issue! However, it is possible to help people in ways that are truly supportive, without invading their privacy or feeling incompetant in dealing with their needs. In *Creative Caring*, Linda and Beth have provided thoughtful, distinct ways in which we can help others, both those close to us and those we don't know as well.

As we try some of the suggestions they provide, we not only learn how to help other men and women in all kinds of circumstances—we experience the gratification of opening up to people who are not that close to us now. We may find that we can help even if we are not in the inner circle of a person's life. In fact, the help of someone who isn't a close friend or family member may be exactly what is needed, especially for people who are experiencing something that frightens those closer to them. For instance, chronically ill people may find relief in unburdening their true feelings without worrying about "laying too much" on their caretakers. And even a small gesture can show a person that we care about them and open the door to more valuable, and relieving, communication.

We reap what we sow. As we open up to others with our help, we find an expansiveness in our own lives and fulfillment in our actions. We find that even when we take time out to help someone else, everything else that we have to do gets done. As we focus on others' difficulties, we put our own problems into perspective. The truth is that no one is exempt from needing help; we all have problems at one time or another. When we feel vulnerable, sad, or worried, we all appreciate considerate support from people we are close to, as well as from those who are beyond our inner circle of friends and relatives. If we have helped others, then we may feel less hesitant to ask for help when we need it. Maybe we will all get better at asking for care as well as giving it.

So thanks to Beth and Linda for bringing us creative and simple ways to show we care, when we are stuck and don't know what to do. We will all be better off.

TAMARA TRAEDER,
co-author of *girlfriends*
July 1997

CHAPTER ONE

Family

Finding time to really care for our families is difficult when we have so many things going on in our lives. Having a strong family base that we can turn to whenever we need it can help us cope with the struggles of everyday life. While every family has its own problems, finding a caring way to relate to one another will allow us to grow stronger.

Many of us feel as though our society is becoming more fragmented, and we find it hard to extend support beyond our family. By giving and receiving support from our neighbors and community, we connect to something larger. We can create the caring society we desire by treating our neighbors as an extended family.

Kindly words, sympathizing attentions, these cost very little but they are priceless in their value. From hour to hour, from moment to moment, we are supported, blest, by small kindnesses.

F. W. ROBERTSON

Challenges of Having a New Baby

Kristen and Kurt were anxious about the arrival of their first baby. They had finished their expectant parent classes and owned almost every book available about giving birth and caring for a newborn. Everyone kept telling them how much their life would change and how they should enjoy their last days as a couple.

Two weeks after the due date, their son finally arrived. None of their reading or classes could have prepared them for how they felt after the birth. Due to a long labor, Kristen was so exhausted she didn't have the stamina to hold the baby.

Each time the infant was brought to her room for feeding, Kristen was nervous. She really didn't know how to hold him or comfort him, and trying to feed him seemed to be a mystery to both of them.

The next day they were discharged from the hospital. They panicked at the thought of being on their own; neither of them had ever changed a diaper. They had taken comfort in being able to push a button and have a knowledgeable person come answer all of their questions.

As they pulled into their driveway, Kristen cried tears of relief and joy at seeing her mother, who had taken a week's vacation to come and stay with them. Kristen's mom helped them into the house, where a pot roast simmered in the oven and fresh bread was rising on the counter.

The first week was tough for Kristen, Kurt, and their son as they got to know one another. Their lack of sleep affected their ability to cope with everyday events. But by the end of the week, both Kristen and Kurt were more confident. The baby was gaining weight, sleeping well, and crying less. As they waved good-bye to Kristen's mother, they were grateful for the week she was there, but they were ready to be on their own.

- ❀ Take a basket of gifts just for the new mother. Have one custom-made or make one yourself with items she likes: her favorite magazines, bath gels, packets of hot chocolate and little miniature candy bars for a snack during those late-night feedings.
- ❀ Give the parents a book to record the gifts they receive. Offer to come back and help address the envelopes for the thank you notes.
- ❀ Offer to take pictures or videos of the family after the delivery and when they arrive home the first day. These will become treasured memories to watch in the weeks and years to come.
- ❀ Take a calendar to friends and family, and ask them to sign up for providing a meal for the first two weeks.
- ❀ Call as often as you can just to offer support and to listen.
- ❀ Bring several disposable cameras for the new parents to

have in various places around the house to catch the baby in all of his or her firsts.

❀ Give the parents information about having a "doula" come in. These services send an experienced mother to help with the new baby, household tasks, and siblings, and they are offered now in most locations.

❀ Be sensitive about visiting too soon. Call and make sure the new parents are up to having someone come to the home. Limit your visit to twenty minutes.

❀ When taking a gift to a new baby, always take one to the older siblings, and have them open theirs first.

❀ Purchase a massage gift certificate for the new parents and baby. Many massage centers now offer baby massages.

❀ Pick up the family's laundry, and return it clean and folded for the first few weeks.

❀ Make dishes of food that are easy to reheat.

❀ Call and send over a pizza for the family.

❀ Not being able to go out socially is very isolating for new parents; offer to "bring in" a social event like a few couples coming over for cards along with a prepared meal.

❀ Call ahead and offer to bring over lunch.

❀ If the new parents don't have a rocking chair, lend or purchase one for them.

For Premature Babies:

❀ When the baby is allowed to go home, offer to come and stay with the baby so the parents can get a break.

❀ Premature babies are not allowed to go out in public until they reach about ten pounds, which in some cases takes several months.

❀ Order a case of premature diapers and have them delivered to their home.

❀ Purchase premature baby clothes, because newborn clothes won't fit for several months.

❀ Locate a support group for parents of preemies.

❀ If you know others who have had a premature baby, ask them to call and share their experiences.

❀ Premature babies have extra doctor visits, so offer to accompany the parents on medical visits.

❀ Call frequently and just listen. New mothers and fathers (especially of preemies) are sometimes overwhelmed and need to have friends who will allow them to share their feelings.

❀ Give new parents disposable cameras so they can take weekly pictures showing their child's progress.

❀ Offer to take the mother and baby for a drive.

❀ Purchase a journal and books on premature births. Suggestion: *Your Premature Baby,* by Frank Manginello, M.D., and Theresa Digeronimo, M.e.D.

Caring for Children

In our hectic lives, it's often hard to find time to spend with those who need it most—children. Research now shows that giving children adequate attention at an early age greatly improves their social and learning skills as they grow up. Children need to know that they are loved and cared for, so here are some ideas for showering attention on the children in your life:

- ❀ Ask if you could take a child out for breakfast on a weekend. This gives parents a chance to have breakfast by themselves or with their other children. Provide an environment for a pleasant breakfast where the child has time to talk with another adult.

- ❀ Send children a postcard every week, just asking how things are going and saying that you're happy to be their friend.

- ❀ Suggest activities children might get involved with outside of school, such as a church choir or sports.

- ❀ Volunteer to stay with the child's siblings while the parents take a day just to spend with the child. Extra attention goes a long way for children.

- ❀ Bring over some little cheer-up treats for the child, such as puzzles, a kite, or an action figure.

- ❀ Find out if there is a special kind of stuffed animal or doll that the child likes. Purchase one and bring it over so that the child knows she or he has a friend.

- Buy tickets for the whole family to get away for a day at the zoo or an adventure park; this gets everybody focused just on fun.
- When visiting, find ways to compliment the children on positive things they are doing.
- Be there for concerned parents as a friend. Raising children is hard, and often they just need a friend for a sounding board.
- Invite a teenager over to your house for a weekend visit to give them a change away from home. Plan movies, eating out, or taking in a sporting event.
- When spending time with teenagers, tell them about your experiences in high school, both the good ones and the bad ones.
- Celebrate even small victories, such as grades improving or making a sports team, by having a special dinner or making or buying a decorated cake.
- Attend children's plays, recitals, and sports events. An audience of true fans and supporters thrills children.
- A gift to any child from a parent could be a handwritten letter about the day the child was born. Include what the parent's feelings were on that day, what the weather was like, who came to visit, how nervous the new parents were.

More Caring for Children

Here are some additional ideas for showering attention on the children in your life:

❀ Purchase coping/encouragement/support cards designed especially for children, and send them often.

❀ Offer to take children shopping for holidays, such as their parents' birthdays, Mother's Day, or Father's Day.

❀ Give a child a cookbook and then plan a few hours to help the child prepare one of the recipes. Only help to the extent the child needs it; let him or her have the fun of figuring things out, and don't worry about the mess.

❀ Set aside time regularly to play board games with children. Most adult games come with junior versions. Play a rousing game of hide-and-seek with younger children.

❀ Plan a movie night and show home movies or videos of the children when they were growing up.

❀ Young children like to be able to help with chores, so enlist their help in measuring foods for dinner and in folding clothes after they come out of the dryer.

❀ Give children their own calendars, and hang them in their rooms. The small ones where you can rip off a page a day are great for young children.

❀ Try to maintain daily rituals, such as reading books at bedtime, eating breakfast together, or cleaning up their room at the end of the day.

❀ Prepare a photo album with pictures from infancy to the present age; children love to see themselves.

❀ Write a letter about why you're glad the child is a part of your life.

❀ Take your children down your memory lane to see the school you attended and the house you grew up in.

❀ Tell children about your nicknames as a child, and tell the story behind the nicknames you've chosen for them.

❀ Help your child learn his or her name in another language.

❀ Put your family on tape—record a whole day.

❀ Have a nonbirthday party on the half-year. Cut a cake in half, and put candles on it.

Special Needs . . . Some Children Need More

Sandy said, "Please finish your breakfast," for what seemed like the hundredth time. The aggravation of trying to get her son, Michael, through breakfast, dressed, and prepared for school usually started the day on a negative note.

Michael had always seemed a little different even as a baby and toddler, but everyone thought it was just a phase he was going through. Family members assumed he would outgrow the behavior and learning problems. When Michael began school, the problems only increased.

He couldn't make friends and hence became a loner standing on the sidelines, never invited to birthday parties and not chosen to be on anyone's team at school. There were also academic problems. Sandy dreaded parent-teacher conferences, knowing she would leave with a list of things that needed attention. At each conference, the messages were the same: Michael didn't pay attention and couldn't focus on his work, and therefore his grades suffered.

Sandy knew she had to do something. She took him to a psychologist who diagnosed Michael with a severe case of ADHD (attention deficit hyperactivity disorder). After carefully weighing her options, she decided to agree to give Michael daily medication to help his hyperactivity.

As the years went by, even though everyone was trying to help Michael, he began to give up. Going to school was a major effort. An environment with no friends and very little positive reinforcement became too much of a burden. Sandy was frustrated with the failure of the school system, which couldn't give him the extra attention he needed.

Sandy finally removed Michael from school and decided to teach him at home. Everyone advised against this, but she felt it was her only hope of providing an environment where Michael could learn. She knew he was bright, and she hoped she would have what it took to teach him. Their days became field trips filled with hands-on nature experiences walking through the woods. A trip to their state capital became a live history lesson. Sandy was thrilled as she found learning opportunities for her son and watched him thrive. She was confident she was on the right path to helping her son grow up to be able to survive in the world.

- ❀ Children with learning disabilities respond well to a one-on-one relationship. Take the child to an event such as a hands-on museum, a puppet show, or a play area where she or he can release some energy.
- ❀ Show the family you care by reading about the problem they are dealing with so you can relate better.
- ❀ Give the parents a gift certificate to a restaurant, and offer to take their children for the evening to give them a well-deserved break.
- ❀ If the child requires outside tutoring, offer your skills in

music or reading.

* Provide information regarding special educational activities, such as making a bird house or taking a bird walk at the local sanctuary.
* Children often relate to animals, so give the family tickets to the zoo.
* Help celebrate successes, such as learning to read or count, with a special cake and candles.
* Throw a get-together for the child and several friends from school in a safe environment such as bumper bowling.
* Browse bookstores or teachers' stores and pick up educational books, puzzles, and workbooks.
* Bring videos that are fun yet provide learning at the same time.
* Bring learning and animation into the child's world with computer CD-ROMs of books, math, or reading.
* Write frequent notes of encouragement to the parents, who are watching their child struggle.
* Offer lots of hugs and holding their hand.
* To recognize the child's efforts, plan a party and let the child make invitations and dessert.

Aging Gracefully

Sharon had tried to keep her sense of humor and a positive outlook about one simple fact: she was getting old. Her body just didn't do the things it used to, no matter how much coaxing she gave it. Sharon knew she needed to accept her body as it was and to learn to live with the changes that were occurring. There was so much more for her to think about than before. Even a simple trip across town to run errands could not be done without having to visit a public restroom at each stop. Lately, running just one errand would leave her exhausted.

She did not like having to make decisions about what she should and shouldn't do, such as whether to have a second cup of coffee, knowing it would cause trouble in half an hour. There was the heartache of having to turn down some of her all-time favorite foods, particularly the garlic-based pasta dish she enjoyed at the local Italian restaurant. The last two times she had eaten it, she had spent most of the night in the bathroom.

Some days when she awakened, it seemed like it would be easier to lie there all day than to deal with her aching muscles. She was aware that she was losing some of her hearing. It was annoying to ask someone to repeat what she or he had said. Her television set needed to be turned louder. She was constantly misplacing her glasses, and she couldn't see without them. She knew her checkbook was not always correct, and she was becoming forgetful about recording each check. She looked at the bottles of pills she had to take for one ailment or another and was surprised that she needed so much medication each day. She tried to keep her positive outlook because she knew that age was something to accept with grace and elegance, but it wasn't easy. . . .

❀ Purchase a journal and encourage an aging person to record just one item per day that he or she is grateful for.

❀ Provide your aging friend with a list of senior exercise classes.

❀ Start a monthly change-the-host get-together. Friends are invited to bring a dish to pass, and a different person hosts the event each month.

❀ Purchase and give a copy of the book *Grow Old Along with Me, the Best Is Yet to Be.*

❀ Purchase a poster stating the sentiment, "You're not getting older, you're getting better."

❀ Obtain a listing of senior social activities in the person's area: dancing, bowling, cards, and games.

❀ Give them a schedule for walking inside the local mall. Attach coupons for coffee after their exercise.

❀ Purchase and frame the poem "When I Am An Old Woman I Shall Wear Purple" and give as a gift.

❀ A gift for seniors could be a gift certificate to a restaurant or an invitation to come over for dinner, even if it's just a sandwich or salad. Seniors enjoy company and a chance to get out of their own house.

❀ Purchase a massage gift certificate for those tired muscles and joints.

❀ Purchase flannel blankets or comforters to keep warm while watching TV or reading. Include a variety of unique and special tea bags for a cup of hot tea.

❀ Encourage your senior friend to find groups, regardless of age, with shared interests such as poetry reading, exercising, volunteering. Spending time with others who are younger helps one feel younger.

❀ Suggest opportunities for volunteering at a local pre-school. Little children love to give smiles and hugs.

❀ Contact a literacy organization and teach someone to read.

❀ Concentrate on accepting the things in life you cannot change. Read *Don't Sweat the Small Stuff . . . and It's All Small Stuff,* by Richard Carlson, Ph.D.

❀ Take time to really look at yourself. Focus on your inner beauty rather than the external parts you would like to change.

Caring for Neighbors

Every day on the news we hear about the breakdown of community. Connecting to those who live in your neighborhood is always a challenge, but it can be a way to help restore a sense of community in your life. All it takes is some simple consideration for your neighbors—doing favors for one another, looking out for one another's property if someone's on vacation, reporting suspicious people in the area. Treat your entire neighborhood as an extension of your house, and you'll soon feel as though you belong to something larger:

❀ When you see your neighbor outside in the yard or at the mailbox, take the time to go over and say "Hi" and "How are you?"

❀ Be aware of people in your neighborhood who might need an extra hand. When you see your elderly neighbor trying to drag bags of leaves or weekly trash to the curb, do it for him or her.

❀ When you order pizza in, order doubles, and take one to the elderly couple down the street who might enjoy a takeout dinner.

❀ When someone new moves to the area, do the traditional thing by going over and introducing yourself, bringing a plate of cookies.

❀ Look for ways that your neighbors could help one another. Can you organize a shared baby-sitting service, so that each parent could get some time off on a regular basis?

- In warm weather, canvass your neighborhood to hold a barbecue or potluck dinner. Ask others to help coordinate. This is a great way for everyone, including the children, to get to know one another better.

- Tune in to what is going on with your neighbors: is someone expecting a baby, or has the couple down the street just gotten married? Drop by with a small gift, or send a note of congratulations.

- Use the holidays to bring neighbors together for celebration. Have a neighborhood pumpkin-decorating contest. Let the children be the judges.

- Organize holiday caroling with members of your neighborhood and visit a local nursing home. Return to someone's home afterward for hot chocolate.

- Get to know your neighbors well enough to know of their special talents, then find ways to use one another's skills. One neighbor may be wonderful at sewing, another may be an expert pie baker, and another may have fix-it skills. Trade services with one another.

- On Friday night when everyone is just too tired to entertain or be social, ask neighbors over anyway. Have everyone bring snacks, then rent the latest videos for the children and adults.

The Instant Family

David and Betty were married in 1966. Eleven months after the wedding, Betty was diagnosed with ovarian cancer. The news was devastating to this young couple just beginning their life together. Betty was told that because of the surgery and chemotherapy, she would not be able to have children. David was told that Betty's chances for survival were slim. But after the surgery, Betty continued to improve and respond to the treatments, so they started discussing the possibility of adopting a child. They were informed by the adoption agency they would have to wait for five years to see if Betty's cancer returned.

After five years of waiting, David and Betty contacted two adoption agencies and were asked questions such as: Would they adopt an older child? Would they consider a child from another race or country? Would they take a child with known medical or mental problems? David and Betty already had pondered these decisions and were ready to proceed. The process began with them being interviewed both individually and together, having their home inspected and sharing their last several years of financial data. Then they waited for three years.

The phone call finally came. They were told they could have a fifteen-month-old African American boy in twenty-four hours if they wanted him. One look in each other's eyes, and Betty and David said yes immediately. The next few hours found them frantically calling their family and friends from church to borrow necessities such as a car seat, high chair, crib and a playpen. Unlike parents who have nine months to prepare both emotionally and physically for a new child, adoptive parents are just on hold, waiting for the call that might not come for years.

As white Presbyterian ministers, they encountered various reactions to their interracial family. While any adoption causes adjustments for both the parents and the child, theirs presented the extra challenges of raising a black child in a nonblack household. Their unconditional love for each other and their child gave them a strong foundation, but they appreciated help from caring people.

- ❀ Throw a baby shower for the parents after they have the child, and give a list of items the baby needs to those who are invited.
- ❀ Provide the parents with items they need to baby-proof their home, and take the time to help install them.
- ❀ Purchase a medical records journal to record the information provided by the adoption agency or the foster home. Information about the child's sleep schedule, eating habits, and likes and dislikes will be very important.
- ❀ Give the parents copies of child care books.
- ❀ Lend the parents baby furniture and a car seat that you aren't using.

❁ Offer to take pictures or videotapes of the child on the day he or she joins the family, and send the photos to relatives who are not able to be there.

❁ If the adopted child is older, give him or her some time to feel comfortable with the new family. Suggest ways to get to know the extended family of grandparents, uncles and aunts, and other cousins, like an afternoon picnic with planned games.

❁ As a friend or relative, spend time with the adopted child on a regular basis so she or he can feel loved by others.

❁ Record the date of the adoption, and send an annual celebration of an anniversary cake or a bunch of balloons.

❁ Give the parents a baby book or journal in which to record the events.

Caring for Everyday Heroes

There are many people in our lives who help us every day without being actively acknowledged. Here are some ideas for taking extra time to show service people that they are cared for in return:

- ❀ People who work in the media often go unrecognized. If a radio personality has helped you publicize an event or has brought attention to a community need, buy a bag of scones and drop off with a thank you note.

- ❀ Make it a point to learn the first name of everyone who serves you. The coffee server at the local coffeehouse would welcome a smile and hearing his or her name in the morning.

- ❀ Acknowledge the person who delivers the mail by leaving a small gift, in your mailbox, like a candy bar or an apple, with a note of thanks.

- ❀ If the same waiter or waitress serves you at your favorite restaurant, leave a rose on the table along with your tip to brighten his or her day.

- ❀ Recognize those who put in endless hours volunteering for nonprofit organizations by doing something to directly support their cause. Maybe you could help solicit donations, make phone calls, or stuff envelopes.

- ❀ When someone treats you courteously, smiles, and goes the extra mile, make sure to tell that person's boss.

- ❀ When you attend a fundraiser that you really enjoyed,

send a letter to the editor of the local newspaper and give kudos for a job well done.

- ❀ Buy a dozen one-dollar lottery tickets to give to the person working at the gas station, to the dry cleaner attendant, and even to the meter reader!

- ❀ Bring the janitor a cake on his or her birthday. Ask everyone in the building to join in a round of "Happy Birthday."

- ❀ For the janitor who faithfully cleans each night, leave a yellow sticky on your desk, saying, "Thank you for doing this every day."

- ❀ Bring your child's music teacher his or her favorite drink to sip at the beginning of the lesson. Many teachers go for hours with no break.

- ❀ For the sports coach who works all day, then volunteers time after work for children, bring snacks and drinks for everyone after practice.

- ❀ Be an active team supporter by volunteering for activities that support the team, like fundraisers for new uniforms.

- ❀ Help your child write a personal thank you note at the end of the season, telling the coach how much she or he enjoyed their coaching.

- ❀ Take dinner in a big picnic basket to your child's caretaker for her or his family to enjoy. After a long day of caring for children, dinner already made will be greatly appreciated.

❀ Find out when your child's teacher's birthday is, then bring in treats that everyone can enjoy with the teacher.

❀ To thank your cleaning person, leave a little gift of appreciation along with a note in the basket with the cleaning supplies.

❀ Recognize your secretary or your support person frequently, not just during the once-a-year Secretary's Day. Thank your assistant sincerely for the tasks he or she does for you.

❀ Give your support staff gift certificates for lunch at the mall, then tell them to take an extra hour for some shopping.

❀ Bring a pot of coffee around in the morning and serve your support group.

More Caring for Neighbors

Here are some more ways to care about your neighbors:

❀ When neighbors visit, have their special kind of beverage available.

❀ Take up a neighborhood collection to send flowers when a neighbor passes away. Have everyone sign a large neighborhood card reminiscing about the person.

❀ Help the neighborhood feel unified by suggesting everyone put a pot of bright red geraniums or yellow poppies on their porch as a symbol.

❀ Have a neighborhood yard sale and donate the money earned to a local charity.

❀ If you know your neighbors have been unusually busy, surprise them by mowing their lawn when you cut your own.

❀ Set up a network so everyone knows when one neighbor is on vacation. Then everyone can watch the vacationer's home, with one designated neighbor getting the mail each day.

❀ If one of your neighbors is chronically ill, volunteer to stay with him or her while the family gets some time away.

❀ If neighbors have invited a lot of relatives to town for a special occasion, like a wedding or reunion, volunteer your extra bedroom for the guests.

- When snowblowing your sidewalk, do your neighbor's as well. For warmer climates, help with planting flowers.
- If you have an empty lot or park nearby, plan a picnic with games.
- Have a neighborhood softball team and play weekly, all ages welcome.
- If you notice neighbors painting or repairing their home, offer to help.
- For winter climates, build one giant neighborhood snowman.

CHAPTER TWO

Illness

Taking care of a sick loved one allows us to show our true colors as friends and family. This is the time when a loved one needs us the most, and we show our love for them through our actions. They find comfort and solace through our support. Our physical state is often directly tied to how we are feeling emotionally, and when a person feels cared for their physical discomfort can be lessened.

The caregiver also benefits from the act of care. As we support an ill person, we are given the gift of knowing that we have positively affected the life of another person. Helping one another when we are in need is part and parcel of being human and helps us understand how we all depend on others. Truly taking care of one another is probably some of the best work we can do. This chapter describes ways we can take care of those people in our lives who are suffering from illness.

If each individual in the world simply did all that was in her or his power each day for the persons whose lives come in natural contact with his or her own, the entire world would be rejuvenated at once.

LILIAN WHITING

Adapting to Asthma

When Matt was a young child, he seemed to always have a cold or respiratory infection. Matt's family had a history of asthma and allergies. The doctors prescribed medication for Matt which needed to be inhaled through a nebulizer machine. This machine takes the medication and creates a mist, which the patient must breathe in through a face mask, helping the bronchial tubes to open.

Matt initially fought having his face covered by a mask and was frightened by the machine. This treatment was stressful for both the parents and Matt, as he had to sit still for about ten minutes. As time passed, Matt adjusted to these treatments, but his parents had be to very creative to find activities for Matt to pass the time.

They took Matt for an allergy test to determine why he was sick so often. The doctor worked fast, pricking each spot with a needle, looking for a reaction The doctor quickly confirmed that Matt was allergic to almost all forty-eight items and, in particular, to environmental factors like dust, mold, trees, grass, and pollen. There was only one test area which showed no reaction—chocolate! Matt's parents were relieved for this small favor and quickly rewarded him for enduring the test with a candy bar of his choice.

It was difficult for Matt to understand his limitations. He couldn't be outside when his father was cutting the grass; he couldn't romp with the neighbor's dog. In the fall, which for children in the Midwest means raking and jumping in leaves, Matt needed to stay indoors. During the holiday season, the family purchased an artificial tree.

Matt's parents are able to provide him many opportunities for enjoying the outside world. Matt attends summer day camp, and the counselors work with his parents to understand Matt's condition. Matt's grandparents live on a farm and he loves to go there and be outside. While visiting the farm, Matt's parents and grandparents monitor his condition more closely and change his medication as needed. The support of relatives and friends allows Matt to have a normal life.

❀ Help the parents of a child with asthma or allergies to be informed by providing information such as brochures from the Asthma Foundation.

❀ Volunteer to become knowledgeable about the child's medical condition and medication needs, so the parents will have at least one qualified person available to take care of the child.

❀ Offer to stay with the child so both parents can attend a local support group for parents of asthmatics.

❀ Look for a listing of national camps available for asthmatic children, where children can attend with other asthmatics to have fun and at the same time to learn more about their illness and how to manage it.

❀ When including someone with allergies in social activities, be sensitive to their special needs. Ask ahead if there are allergies and if there is anything you should do before the family visits your home.

❀ Ask parents what gifts you should avoid purchasing for a child who has allergies or asthma. For instance, children with these conditions should not have stuffed animals because of the dust that collects in them.

❀ Give the child coloring books, crayons, puzzles, or hand-held games, which the child can use while taking the treatment.

❀ Prepare a few short art projects that will take about ten minutes and give these to the child to do during treatments.

❀ Give the child some pop-up books to explore during treatment.

❀ If children are unable to be in certain environments like the country or a farm, bring these in to them through the world of video or an interactive CD-ROM.

❀ Volunteer to go to the child's school and put on a demonstration for the class on what asthma is and how it is treated.

Caring for Someone Who Is Sick

No matter what kind of illness someone has, from a cold to pneumonia, getting extra attention is especially needed when we are feeling under the weather. Being cared for is sometimes the only thing that can brighten a day spent in bed. Many people think that getting loving attention can actually help one heal. Following are some ideas for giving someone ill the attention they truly need:

* Offer comfort to someone with a cold or flu by bringing soup, tissues, and some magazines.

* For a friend on crutches, arrange to drive him or her to work or school. Buy your friend a backpack to carry personal items in.

* For someone having eye surgery, deliver a bouquet of fragrant flowers or a gardenia plant.

* For a child having ear or tonsil surgery, send a walking balloon to the home or hospital room.

* If someone is having outpatient surgery, offer to provide a ride to the hospital and back home. Stay with the person for a while at home if you can.

* For a co-worker who has been off work with a minor illness, offer to collect mail and handle messages. Phone her or him at home and ask if there are any details that you could handle in the office.

* Welcome co-workers back with a bouquet or take them out to lunch. Often people feel guilty when they miss

work and have anxiety about returning.

- ❀ If people come to work who clearly should be at home for their own comfort and the health of their co-workers, make arrangements for someone to handle their work, and encourage them to leave.

- ❀ For a friend recovering from foot surgery, pay a visit at home. Bring videos and library books to keep him or her busy.

- ❀ Make sure someone ill has access to a cordless phone, especially if that person lives alone. Lend yours or purchase one as a gift.

- ❀ Almost anyone ill can feel cheered with the gift of a cuddly stuffed animal.

- ❀ For friends who are in bed with a short-term illness, offer to walk or feed their pets.

- ❀ When you know someone who can't get out for a few days, call and ask what you can pick up for that person at the store.

- ❀ Offer to take a sick friend's children for the day or evening to allow them to rest.

- ❀ Someone ill may not feel like eating, but offer to bring by a meal for the rest of the family.

- ❀ Send a card, even for a minor illness.

- ❀ Bring some new tapes or CDs of music an ill friend would enjoy to help pass the time, for a change from reading and watching television.

❀ Fix meals that can be microwaved easily, and put them in single-serving containers.

❀ Ask your ill friend if he or she would enjoy some books on tape, then check some out of the library and drop them off.

❀ Take combs and brushes or nail polish and help your friend fix hair or nails. Or give a backrub to soothe and refresh your friend's body.

❀ For someone recovering from eye surgery, help them highlight their television guide for the shows they want to watch. This keeps eye strain to a minimum.

❀ Donate blood at the Red Cross for a friend who is hospitalized.

❀ Donate some of your vacation days to someone who is off work due to illness.

❀ When visiting someone who is ill or hospitalized call and ask the best time to visit. Limit visits to twenty minutes.

The Mystery of a Medical Test

Liz and Jim, in their early forties, wanted a second child. Liz's pregnancy was more difficult this time; she was sick and more uncomfortable the first few months. The obstetrician suggested that they have prenatal testing because with Liz's age, there were greater possibilities of birth defects. What would they do if the results of the test suggested their baby would not be normal and healthy? What assurance could they have in the tests being accurate? Through reading, research, and prenatal counseling, Liz and Jim found solace in knowing that today's tests could screen out severe chromosomal abnormalities.

They elected to have a test procedure done at ten weeks' gestation, in order to have the information early. Liz and Jim were somewhat uncomfortable about having the procedure done because it seemed rather invasive, but after talking at length with the doctor, they decided to go ahead. Thirty minutes later, they watched the tiny ten-week-old embryo on the ultrasound screen.

During the procedure, the doctor had difficulty getting a sample of the placenta that would be analyzed later for chromosomal makeup. Three times he tried to obtain a sample with a pincerlike instrument, but finally he told Liz and Jim he was unable to get a biopsy. As Liz watched the screen during this process, she was surprised at the depth of her emotions each time the embryo moved. After enduring the anxiety of making the decision to have the procedure done, they couldn't believe there would now be no results.

Weeks passed, and the thought of the test began to fade from memory until Liz started to bleed. Having previously miscarried, she panicked and drove to the doctor's office. An ultrasound confirmed a hole in the placenta, probably caused by the test procedure.

Liz was resigned to bedrest until the bleeding stopped, perhaps till the end of the pregnancy. She had risked her own health and that of her baby's for the test. She felt guilty for going through with the procedure. But the real agony was knowing that for twenty-eight more weeks, she would not know if the baby was okay. The days and weeks of bedrest and mental anguish were rewarded when Liz delivered a healthy son at the end of the pregnancy.

❀   For parents-to-be facing pregnancy complications, gather material on prenatal conditions so they can be informed about what is going on.

❀   Provide the mother-to-be with a list of other mothers with similar situations so that they can talk with one another. The doctor's office could help in connecting them.

❀   Encourage the pregnant woman to contact others who have been through this experience.

❀   For a pregnant woman confined to bedrest, suggest she

invite a new mother and baby over for a visit, to be reminded of the wonderful outcome there will be after the pregnancy is over and the baby has arrived.

❀ Help organize the room where the pregnant woman is staying so that she can be as active as possible and do things for herself.

❀ Purchase a cable TV service so that a bedridden pregnant woman can choose from a variety of programs.

❀ Volunteer to do chores that she normally did, such as grocery shopping.

❀ Find out if the mother-to-be used to enjoy handwork, like knitting or crocheting, and bring her a kit to allow her to take up this hobby again now that she has time on her hands.

❀ Organize some special activities or projects that the children and their bedridden mom can do together. This helps to make special time for children who may be confused by their mother not getting out of bed to play with them.

❀ If she enjoys makeup, bring her a tray of nail colors and lipsticks she can experiment with.

❀ Buy her a journal, and encourage her to write about her feelings.

❀ Install a phone jack in her bedroom so that she can use her modem for faxes, e-mail, or the Internet.

❀ Bring *Gone with the Wind* to help pass the time.

Chronic Illness Takes Courage

After graduating from high school in 1970, Linda developed a fever and nausea and lost twenty-five pounds. She couldn't accept the diagnosis of flu, so she consulted a specialist who told her she had Crohn's disease (inflammatory bowel disease.) The pain, internal bleeding, medication side effects, and endless trips to the hospital for tests was overwhelming for an eighteen-year-old. Yet the real burden was not the illness or the bleak prognosis, but the lack of support she needed to accept and understand the illness.

A real challenge for chronically ill people is they may "look fine" but inside they may be feeling lousy. In addition to coping with physical distress, they must deal with the worry and sense of vulnerability that being ill brings with it. The future is not a topic that can be discussed; it is difficult enough to get through today, this week, and this month. Linda must cope with the innocent thoughtlessness of others, who do not understand her limitations. There are days and weeks when Linda is not able to eat, and people make silly remarks such as, "Are you on a diet?" Sometimes people are reluctant to acknowledge her illness, thinking they might somehow "catch it."

Linda's physician has given her courage, support, and a shoulder to cry on for more than twenty years. But the greatest gift he gave her was suggesting that she begin a support group to help others. She accepted the challenge and has been holding monthly meetings for five years. Linda finds counseling others as therapeutic for her as it is for them. Knowing how important information can be, Linda provides books, videos, and pamphlets to others with chronic illness. She offers a listening ear any time of the day or night. She recently spent time talking with a man who was facing surgery for his ulcerative colitis. He had called her because he needed to talk to someone who had faced similar decisions about surgery. Volunteering to help others is the most rewarding work she has ever done. Giving someone a few minutes or an hour of your time to listen and empathize is truly a gift from the heart.

❀ Make a contribution to the organization that sponsors research toward a cure, such as the Crohn's and Colitis Foundation of America. The organization will acknowledge your gift to the patient.

❀ Send a donation to the organization in a birthday card to them each year.

❀ When a friend is going to the hospital for extensive tests, ask if she or he is going alone, and if so, accompany your friend if you can. An ill person's family is not always available or would prefer not to because they may be having a hard time dealing with their anxiety or fear.

❀ Take a cassette player with headphones and relaxation tapes along for your friend to listen to while waiting for medical procedures. Hospitals tend to make people nervous, and reading is sometimes difficult when you are preoccupied with the upcoming procedure.

❁ After the tests, simply be there for your friend; a touch to the hand speaks volumes. Suggest going out for coffee to allow your friend to confide feelings.

❁ If someone you know is hospitalized or home ill, support his or her immediate family by organizing co-workers, friends, or neighbors to bring dinner in nightly.

❁ If an ill friend of yours has a child, attend that child's play or sports event, and videotape it for the parent to see later. Some hospitals will allow you to bring in videos and watch them in your room. This helps the ill person feel a part of his or her child's activities during a very stressful period.

❁ Make a point to call a chronically ill friend at least once a month, and ask how the person really is doing. Follow the call up by sending an encouragement card to let your friend know how much you enjoyed talking and that you're "there for them."

❁ During days where you know they're not doing their best, leave a "pick-me-up" gift at their door, such as a bouquet of flowers, a new book, or a wrapped box of chocolates.

❁ If their illness affects their eating, find out what type of foods they can eat, then make an appropriate dish to take over. When one's food choices are limited, it always taste better if prepared by someone else.

❁ Employ a cleaning service to come in and help out until the person is feeling better.

❁ Inquire as to your friend's favorite author(s), then visit the library and pick up the books they have available.

❁ If the illness prohibits the person from exercising, find out if swimming is an option, then arrange for the person to attend some classes at a local health club.

❁ Make a date to bring a video, and watch it with your friend.

❁ Research the appropriate support groups and give the information to a friend. Offer to go with them the first time.

❁ Ask the person what his or her favorite dessert is, then prepare it or order it from the bakery.

❁ Designate a spokesperson to return calls, provide medical updates, and advise others of what might be needed, such as food or rides.

❁ Coordinate the children's schedules so they have transportation to activities.

Helping Someone with Alzheimer's Cope

Teresa stared at the man across the breakfast table. She couldn't believe it had happened again. She simply could not remember who this man was. Teresa, seventy-four years old, was scared because she knew what was happening. It was starting for her, as it had for her own mother years ago.

It didn't seem to matter how many years had passed since her mother's death; time had not erased the memories Teresa had of caring for her aging mother who suffered from Alzheimer's. The illness was not as well known then as it is today. People made the assumption that when they got old they became forgetful. Today we understand more about this disease that robs people of their ability to reason and remember. Teresa knew firsthand what a ravaging impact it could have on one's life.

When her mother turned sixty-nine, it was clear to the family that her situation had gone from simple forgetfulness to something more severe. The doctor informed the family that their mother had Alzheimer's, and they met to decide what to do. Their mother could not go on living alone, for her memory had faded to the point where she was no longer safe. Reports would come to one of them almost on a daily basis from neighbors who had seen their mother wandering through the neighborhood lost, not knowing who she was or where she lived. It was finally decided that Teresa's house and family was the best place for their mother to live. For the next seventeen months, Teresa's mother lived with her, her husband, and their two teenaged children.

Looking back and remembering, Teresa painfully recalled these months as being long and wearing. Every day began with a fight with her mother. She didn't want to get up or get dressed, she didn't want to eat her dinner, she didn't know who Teresa was or why she kept asking her to do things. As the months went by, things worsened; her mother became bitter, defiant, and uncontrollable.

They couldn't leave her alone, so the whole family adjusted their schedules so that someone could always be home with Grandma. For Teresa and her husband, it became a real struggle to be a couple, as it seemed they never went anywhere together, including to their children's events. They realized their original plan wasn't working. When they weren't arguing with Teresa's mother, they were arguing among themselves. Teresa felt she had to keep some kind of family normalcy, and her mother would need to be cared for in a different way.

She reconvened another meeting with her siblings, and they agreed the only thing to do was to put their mother in a nursing home. They selected a home in their area that took patients with various stages of Alzheimer's. Touring the nursing home that day was a chilling experience for the entire family. They saw things they hoped would not happen to their mother, yet they knew this was reality for some patients with Alzheimer's.

Teresa continued almost daily visits to her mother in the nursing home. She would come and sit next to her and talk to her. Many days Teresa felt she was only talking to herself. Her mother had no recollection of who Teresa was or who she was talking about. Some days when Teresa visited, her mother would sit quietly, and other times she would be in a rage over things that she imagined were happening to her.

While some days it was tough, Teresa continued her vigil of daily visits. Months later, her mother became physically weak, so Teresa simply sat and held her hand. It was almost easier watching her this way. With her eyes closed, she looked more like the mother Teresa wanted to remember, the mother who had a strong mind and body. During the last week of her mother's life, Teresa was there visiting. She was holding her mother's hand, when her mother suddenly opened her eyes, spoke Teresa's name, and said, "Everything will be okay." Those were her mother's last words. In that moment, Teresa knew that her mother knew who she was. She was glad she had continued her daily bedside vigil to hear her last words.

Now, Teresa was looking across the table at her husband, and she knew that what had struck her mother was also beginning to happen to her. Again, she was frightened.

❊ Help an Alzheimer's patient keep a routine to make the day seem normal, such as getting dressed and eating at consistent times.

- Arrange for a hair stylist to come to the house and do their hair.
- Place their bed or chair by a window. Sunlight can help to improve health and disposition.
- Keep a vase with fresh flowers near the bedside.
- If you are a friend or relative of the patient, visit often and talk to the person about her or his past. Many patients can recall memories from their past.
- If the patient must go to a nursing home, discuss with the caregiver what items the patient can have, such as a special food, plants, or books.
- Read the progress and research being done for new drugs and possible cures for the illness, and pass these on to the patient and family.
- Discuss with family members the genetic correlation of Alzheimer's. An open discussion can help adult children better understand their potential to develop the illness.
- Plan activities for the patient, such as art projects and singing familiar songs. Be creative in ways to entertain them, and help them to use their mind instead of sitting and watching TV.
- Call ahead to let the patient know you're coming to visit; make sure it is a good time. Bring only one other person, so it will not be overwhelming for the patient to remember everyone's name.
- If the patient doesn't have a pet, bring an affectionate

animal over for a visit, such as a cat, rabbit, or small dog. Most patients really connect with an animal.

❀ Bring picture albums you have of your family, and go through them during your visit with the patient, reminding the person of who people are.

❀ Discuss with grandchildren (if they are old enough) what has happened to grandma or grandpa.

❀ If the Alzheimer's patient is a parent, be sure to have the person's legal documents, such as a will, in order, and give each child a copy.

❀ Come over and take the patient out for a ride in the country or to a lake or maybe a park.

❀ Bring soothing music that you think they might enjoy.

❀ Bring over some Disney adventure movies for them to enjoy.

❀ Buy a sleeping mask to close out the light when he or she needs an afternoon nap.

❀ Books that could help: *Failure-Free Activities for the Alzheimer's Patient,* by Carmel Sheridan, *The Alzheimer's Sourcebook for Caregivers,* by Frena Gray Davidson, and *Alzheimer's: Finding the Words,* by Donna Cohen, Ph.D., and Carol Eisdorfer, Ph.D., M.D.

When Cancer Invades Your Life

Cathy had the feeling something was not right. She had just celebrated her forty-second birthday and remembered that this was the same age her mother had been when diagnosed with breast cancer.

Cathy had had her annual exam, including her mammogram, only weeks before and had been given a clean bill of health. But she noticed a change in the look of her breast and knew in her heart that something was wrong. She was referred to the breast clinic at the university for a second opinion. There they performed a needle biopsy, which was a very painful test. After the biopsy, the physician told Cathy she had Stage III breast cancer, which is quite serious given that Stage V is fatal.

She had another biopsy surgery which showed that the cancer had metastasized and therefore a mastectomy would be required. Before the surgery, Cathy underwent two months of chemotherapy treatments on a weekly basis. She ended up asking for a six-month medical leave from work, leaving a job that she really enjoyed. But she found that the isolation of staying home gave her too much time to worry about what was happening. Her family felt awkward and didn't know how to help. The treatments made her exhausted. She had difficulty even doing the simplest tasks like preparing a meal. During that time, her hair fell out. She finally asked her husband to shave her head so she wouldn't keep losing clumps of hair.

In the two months before the surgery, Cathy made radical changes in her lifestyle. She committed her life to God, quit smoking, exercised daily, practiced meditation, took vitamins, and changed her diet. When she went in for her checkup prior to surgery, the doctors were stunned at how much the tumor had shrunk in those two months. They were not sure if it was the chemotherapy or the lifestyle changes but concluded it was probably a combination of both. Cathy has been cancer free for three years now. She is convinced that her positive attitude and desire to live a full life are why she is alive today.

- ❀ Give books on cancer to your friend as soon as possible after the diagnosis.
- ❀ If you live out of town, plan a visit to your friend or family member.
- ❀ Try to go to a doctor appointment with your friend.
- ❀ For a woman who has lost her hair due to chemo-therapy, give her scarves, turbans, and even funny hats to wear.
- ❀ Be a friend who tells jokes, brings over funny movies, and keeps the patient's spirits up.
- ❀ Give the patient a journal, and encourage him or her to write about feelings daily.
- ❀ Purchase a copy of *Fine Black Lines: Reflections on Facing*

Cancer, Fear and Loneliness, by Lois Tschetter Hjelmskad.

❀ Provide radio headphones to pass the time while waiting for treatment at the hospital.

❀ Take meals to the patient, especially on chemotherapy days. Ask first what the person will be able to tolerate. Chemo makes most patients ill, and bland food may be all they can eat.

❀ Make a special ritual of going out with the patient the day before the treatment for a movie, walk in the park, or coffee with a favorite dessert.

❀ The day of the treatment, acknowledge the patient's feelings by giving him or her a small gift like a book, special card with a note, or flowers.

❀ Celebrate the last day of chemotherapy with a party of cake and sparkling juice. Take pictures.

❀ When you visit a patient who has lost his or her hair, bring funny hats such as coneheads or clowns that you can both wear. Have your friend pose with you as someone takes pictures. These will be treasured in years to come.

❀ Give the patient a plastic pill box to keep track of medications.

❀ Give the patient a new robe or pajamas.

❀ Purchase a clip-on book light for night reading.

❀ Bring a jigsaw or crossword puzzle, and work on it with the patient.

Embracing the Time We Have Together

Robert and his family were distraught when his father was diagnosed with leukemia. His previously normal life took a drastic turn that now included frequent doctor visits and blood transfusions. Robert's father was a patient, kind man who always saw the best in his son. He loved his daughter-in-law and delighted in getting to know his grandson.

Robert felt frustrated knowing his father was not going to improve. Because they lived so far away, it was hard to be supportive. Robert's wife suggested he give his father a mailbox on their voicemail system. A week later, they gave him an 800 number and a list of instructions on how to receive and leave messages. Now, Robert could leave a message for his father any time he wanted to, relieved that he wouldn't be calling at a time when he was sleeping or not up to having a conversation.

Robert's dad enjoyed checking each day for his messages. Robert would leave him updates about things he was working on as an engineer. Sometimes he would ask his father for advice on what he was designing. Sometimes he would relay news that he felt his dad would be interested in because he had lived in that part of the country. Their daily messages became a ritual that helped them stay connected at a very difficult time. Knowing that each message left for his father could be the last helped Robert choose his words. It now seemed very normal and comfortable to say, "Thanks, I needed to hear that from you, I really need your advice," or a simple, "I love you, Dad." By maintaining frequent communication, in addition to other support offered by friends and family, Robert's father's final months were filled with love.

- ❀ Donate blood earmarked for the patient, especially if he or she needs blood transfusions on a regular basis.
- ❀ Many who are at home rent hospital beds for the convenience it offers. Help make a hospital bed more festive by decorating the rails or purchasing colored sheets. Try to get the deep-pocketed sheets that will stay on as the position of the bed is changed.
- ❀ Patients who are homebound still like to receive visitors. Provide an environment for visiting that is comfortable for the patient as well as the visitors. You might set up the hospital bed in the living room instead of the bedroom. Try to place it near a window. Place chairs around for visitors to sit in.
- ❀ Purchase some relaxation clothes, such as a pair of sweats or flannel pajamas that don't look like pajamas, so the patient can be comfortable, yet dressed when visitors come over.
- ❀ Encourage the patient to get dressed each day, regardless of whether visitors are expected. Dressing for the day can help lift a patient's spirits.

- Bring takeout food from a favorite restaurant when patients are unable to leave their home.

- Take them "out to the movies" by picking up a new video and bringing popcorn or ice cream.

- Send letters frequently, even if they're short. Include an interesting article you clipped from the paper. When you're in bed all day, getting "real" mail is important.

- Send them a new magazine subscription.

- Make videotapes of what's going on with your life. A video of your garden or changing seasons is a good idea. The focus is on taking the time to make a tape and send it, regardless of your photographic talents.

- Contact a hospice group to help everyone cope.

- Ask the patient if there are family or friends you could keep up-to-date on their condition.

- Spend time discussing with the patient what plans have been made for their care.

- Help the person prepare a will and power of attorney forms.

- Purchase a copy of *The Power of Positive Thinking,* by Normal Vincent Peale.

Caring for a Caregiver

Taking care of someone who needs constant attention is extremely difficult and energy consuming. Full-time caregivers need to know that they are not alone in their responsibilities; they need to feel support as they support their loved one. Here are some ways for you to acknowledge the sacrifice and commitment of a caregiver:

❀ Send coupons for restaurants (be sure they have carry-out service) so the caregiver can pick up a meal and bring it home.

❀ If you live far from a relative who is ill and cannot visit often, make efforts to stay in touch with the caregiver. Call once a week and find out how the week was for that person.

❀ If the caregiver works full-time while assuming responsibility for the patient, send flowers at work to brighten his or her day. Consider doing this on a monthly basis.

❀ If the caregiver has siblings, encourage them to get together and discuss what everyone in the family can do to lessen the burden for the caregiver. Maybe a relative can drive the patient to doctor or dentist appointments or do the shopping once a week.

❀ Give the caregiver a break by offering to stay with the patient for a few hours so he or she can go out to dinner, shopping, or to a movie.

❀ Offer to stay with the patient for a week and give the

caregiver a vacation. This might be the only way she or he can have time off.

❀ Call and tell the caregiver you're coming over to help. Then, when you arrive, get out the vacuum, empty wastebaskets, load the dishwasher, and change the sheets.

❀ Bring groceries for the caregiver. Ask what perishables are needed, and pick those up also.

❀ Bring movies that the caregiver would enjoy watching while sitting with the patient.

❀ Frequently send cards or write notes to caregivers. They appreciate words of encouragement.

❀ If the caregiver comes in for the day, pick up dinner for them to take home to their family.

❀ Give theater, movie, or sporting event passes to the caregiver.

❀ Bring CDs or taped music the caregiver would enjoy listening to during the day.

❀ Give the caregiver a gift certificate for a massage, since taking care of someone else can be physically fatiguing.

❀ Purchase a room monitor, like those available for babies' nurseries. This allows the caregiver to be in the kitchen or to leave the house for a few minutes to get the newspaper, and still be able to hear through the monitor if the patient needs help.

❀ Offer to bring lunch in, and stay to eat it with the caregiver and possibly the patient. This provides some time for everyone to socialize.

❀ In the evening, offer to come over with ice cream and toppings to make sundaes.

❀ Have a visiting nurse service available to relieve the caretaker of some of the medical responsibilities. Often, they can assist in moving and bathing the patient, changing the sheets, and so forth.

❀ Find out the caregiver's birthday and plan a party for him or her with cake and balloons.

❀ Take photos of the patient and caregiver and frame one of them.

❀ Make plans to take the patient and caregiver out to breakfast occasionally.

❀ If the caregiver's duties include transporting the patient, be sure the vehicle is safe and convenient.

Hospice Brings Dignity

Mary and her brother, Ken, loved their mother and could not believe the end was near. It had been several years of watching the cancer eat away at Elizabeth's body and soul.

When the diagnosis of cancer was made a few years earlier, Elizabeth and her family were in disbelief. Mary and Ken had always been close and were blessed with relatives who were always there for them. So they decided to take turns caring for their mother and, if necessary, to put their careers on hold.

Mary took a Family Medical Leave from her job to care for her mother. Ken offered to help with evenings and weekends so Mary could spend time with her own family. They realized they were unprepared to cope with the sudden turn Elizabeth's disease was taking and the demands it made upon them.

After careful deliberation, they decided to contact the local hospice organization. A hospice team understands the mechanics of saying good-bye to loved ones, and the volunteers who visited Elizabeth were willing to help. The hospice movement regards dying as part of the natural flow of life. It borrows its name from travelers' havens during the Middle Ages; hospice is the final way station on the pilgrimage from life to death. Mary and Ken were fortunate that Elizabeth had Medicare insurance, but all patients are accepted into the program regardless of their ability to pay.

Family members are urged to help with the patient's care, with the emphasis on *caring* rather than curing. Hospice has been described as "encircling arms around a family in crisis." The hospice volunteer would arrive to take over for a few hours, giving Mary and Ken the time they needed to go out for coffee and discuss the next plan of action.

When the day came that Elizabeth died, Mary and Ken were comfortable that she had died peacefully at home and she was not alone or afraid. They reminisce now about all the special days they were able to share with her at the end.

❀ Bring the patient photo albums to browse through while resting.

❀ If you are a friend or relative, offer to stay with the patient for a few hours to allow the caregiver a break.

❀ Find out the patient's favorite food, and have it prepared or delivered on a weekly basis.

❀ Be supportive of the patient's relationship with the medical professionals. Don't question patients' choices if they are content with their care.

❀ Provide bedside water and crackers, and replenish frequently for freshness. Bring spring or sparkling waters for a change. For keeping lips moist, purchase glycerin sticks or lip gloss.

❀ When the patient is having visitors, provide snacks for everyone to share.

- Allow your loved ones to cry, and instead of questioning what's wrong, just offer a hug and a smile.
- Go with the patient to the physician's office, and take notes if necessary on medications and the next appointment. Write them down for the patient when you return.
- Listen, without passing judgment, to the patient's fears, dreams, and complaints, big or small.
- Give the patient a small tape recorder and copies of his or her favorite music.
- Give the gift of a large calendar for the wall and a clock with large numbers for their bedside.
- Bring copies of comedy movies and watch them with the patient. Laughter can help reduce pain and stress in everyone.
- Offer to wash and style the patient's hair.
- Bring your magazines and catalogs for the patient to browse.
- Offer to help address birthday and other special occasion cards. Have the patient sign their name, then address and stamp them.
- If appropriate, arrange to rent a hospital bed that allows the patient to control the height of bed and the positions.
- Discuss with the patient their wishes for their funeral. Write these down and be sure all family members receive a copy.

Granting a Loved One's Final Wish

Mark and Gina were happy. Their son, Greg, was in high school and their daughter, Brooke, had just started college. Mark had a well-paying job that he enjoyed, and Gina worked at a law office. They relished the time they had together as a family.

Mark had hemophilia, a male hereditary blood defect characterized by delayed clotting of the blood, which had been passed on by his mother. Mark took the usual precautions when he was injured or had any contact with blood, knowing that even with a minor injury, he could begin to hemorrhage without being able to control it. Mark had to give himself regular injections of Factor 8 (blood byproducts and saline) to help his blood clotting.

The current newsletter of the National Hemophilia Foundation discussed a test that was being done to see if hemophiliacs had developed the AIDS virus through their blood transfusions. Mark was not concerned, but he and Gina went for testing. To Mark's surprise, he found out he had contracted the virus. As time passed, the virus forced Mark to file for disability. He became too ill and tired to go out with his children.

When winter came to Michigan that year, Mark seemed especially depressed by the dark, cold days. Gina knew his dream was to visit Hawaii. Gina suggested they should simply sell their house and possessions and move to Hawaii. This lifted

Mark's spirits, and he was touched by this loving gesture from Gina. Their family and friends hosted a going-away party for them, a Hawaiian luau with festive foods, drinks, and flower leis for everyone.

They found Hawaii to be full of caring and kind people. The members of a local church supported them with continuous visits and words of encouragement. Two months after arriving in Hawaii, Mark passed away peacefully in his sleep. When Gina and the children returned to Michigan, their house had not yet sold, so they moved back into it. Moving back into the home they had all shared together gave them a comforting sense of being close to Mark.

* Invite the family over for dinner often. If the patient is not able to come, send a plate home for her or him.
* Organize a "Share the Care" program. Call a first meeting of friends and family who might be willing to help. For more information, read the book *Share the Care: How to Organize a Group to Care for Someone Who Is Seriously Ill,* by Cappy Capossela and Sheila Warnock.
* Emotional support is crucial to the well-being of the patient and their family. Provide it through gestures of written notes, encouragement cards, and words during your call.
* Keep the children's teachers and counselor informed of the progression of the illness.

- ❀ For someone weakened with a virus, take over nourishing pots of homemade soup and prepared fresh fruit.
- ❀ Encourage the ill person to spend as much time with the family as possible. If the children want to be near their parent, put up a cot in the parent's room so they can sleep there.
- ❀ Take older children to at least one of the doctor appointments or treatments at the hospital so they can understand what is happening.
- ❀ Discuss with children that hospice caregivers will be part of the dying process.
- ❀ For a very ill person, have a lawyer make a home visit to discuss the legal documents that will be necessary for the family.
- ❀ Discuss with the person's physician what kind of intervention the family wants, such as life support.
- ❀ If the person will need blood transfusions, ask friends or relatives to donate.
- ❀ Find out if your community has a place for grieving children to meet and offer one another support on a regular basis.
- ❀ If children have lost a parent, spend time with them talking, taking them to sporting events, and just going for a walk with them.

Caring for a Community Member in Need

Having friends and family rally around you during a rough time can be the thing that gets you through. A community thrives when each of its members is cared for. Make sure you let someone in need know you are thinking about them and supporting them through their difficult period:

❀ Hold a community meeting for those who want to support a family in need. Together brainstorm everything that could be done, then have volunteers lead each activity.

❀ Make a list of maintenance and household chores that must be done, like general housekeeping, lawn mowing, snow shoveling (if in a cold climate), and house repairs. Friends and family can decide who will do each chore and when.

❀ Make a roster of who will bring meals daily. Make sure the designated person also brings perishables such as lettuce, milk, and fresh bread.

❀ If there are financial needs, like medical expenses or children's education, decide on an appropriate fundraiser.

❀ Solicit services from local businesses that could assist the family, such as a bank officer coming to the home to help with finances, a pharmacist who would make home deliveries, a counselor who would donate time to meet with the family at home.

- ❀ Volunteer to be the family spokesperson to give others updates about the family.

- ❀ Ask a flower shop to donate a fresh bouquet weekly.

- ❀ Show community support by tying colored ribbons to clothing, cars, or trees.

- ❀ Help families direct their grief or sadness toward positive change, such as planting a tree in a loved one's memory or working on changing laws or education.

- ❀ In small communities, leave flyers regarding what has occurred and asking for any specific help required.

- ❀ Let children help by planning and hosting their own fundraiser: a lemonade stand, a bingo game, or work projects.

- ❀ Contact community agencies that can offer support, such as United Way, Red Cross, food banks, domestic abuse shelters, and so forth.

- ❀ See if local schools would take on a project, providing the volunteers and work to plan/coordinate. A group fundraising project might be a bake sale, car wash, or walk/run-athon.

- ❀ Organize a collection of items needed to help those who are permanently or temporarily homeless due to flood, fire, or other natural disaster.

- ❀ Offer to find housing for relatives and friends who are in town.

CHAPTER THREE

Loss

There is nothing more difficult than watching someone you care about cope with a loss. Every loss is traumatic, and it's important that people take the time they need to grieve in their own way. The best thing you can do is be there for them when they need it. Though you may feel powerless in the face of their sorrow, you will help them more than you can imagine by just letting them know how much you care, and that you have empathy for them.

People experiencing a loss need to know that they are not alone. Offering your support to them can help give them the strength they need to experience their grief without becoming consumed by it. This chapter contains ways for you to help someone work through a loss.

Your greatest pleasure is that which rebounds from hearts that you have made glad.

H. W. BEECHER

Losing a Parent

Bonnie had always enjoyed a special relationship with her father. When she thought back to her childhood memories, one of her favorites was their vacation in Florida. Her father found as much fun in the journey as in the destination. So their long trips across the country were broken up by stops at tourist attractions, with a fun evening of swimming at a hotel after a long day in the car.

Bonnie was seventeen when her parents divorced. She was glad they finally ended their constant silent feud. After the divorce, her father bought a house on a lake and seemed to be at peace with himself. His philosophy was to live now, not wait for retirement. He loved to travel, and this enthusiasm and love of life spilled over to Bonnie's life as well.

Last year, Bonnie couldn't be with her dad on Father's Day, so she went a week earlier to visit him. They spent a wonderful weekend going to a movie, grilling fresh fish, and enjoying a leisurely boat ride. Bonnie noticed that her dad was having trouble hearing.

Days later, he still couldn't hear, so he went for tests at a clinic. He was given a clean bill of health except that his blood pressure was slightly elevated, so he went back to work. His secretary brought him the usual big stack of mail and he thumbed through it, picking out a letter from Bonnie, which he opened first. He smiled when he read the letter, expressing how sorry she was that she couldn't spend Father's Day with him this year. She ended it by telling him how much she loved him.

That letter was the last piece of mail he read. While eating lunch, he suffered a cerebral hemorrhage and was rushed to the hospital. When Bonnie arrived, she was told he wouldn't regain consciousness. She could see him if she wanted, but he would not know she was there. Bonnie sat in the waiting room for hours while family and friends arrived. She watched as they all went in to say good-bye. Everyone insisted that Bonnie go in to see him, but she just couldn't. She went to the chapel and prayed about her decision. She wanted to always remember him the way he was only a week earlier—laughing, smiling, hugging her, and calling her "sweetie."

※ Be respectful of the ways others show or hide their grief. We all grieve in different ways and at different times.

※ Make a donation to a charitable organization in memory of the loved one. Continue to do this every year on the anniversary of the death.

※ If the deceased had a family with children, make a donation in that person's name for a college fund.

※ Offer to help the family with the paperwork involved in notifying insurance companies, the Social Security office, and other businesses.

- Nominate a friend or relative who can field the inquiries when there has been a tragic accident. It is difficult for immediate family members to have to keep telling others what happened.
- If the immediate family owns a family business, offer to stay and watch over the business during the memorial services.
- Send a tribute, such as the traditional arrangement of flowers, or consider planting a tree, creating a picture collage, or writing a poem.
- Gently encourage the grieving family to take rest and nourishment.
- Help family members talk about their final wishes, and be sure that everyone understands their plans.
- Consider having a living will for yourself as well as your loved ones.
- Sign an organ donor card, and encourage your family and friends to do the same, so those waiting will live from an organ transplant.
- Relay a memory of the loved one to family members.
- A book to help one understand the stages of grief is *Losing a Parent,* by Alexandra Kennedy.
- A good journal is *I Remember You: A Grief Journal,* by Layner Wild.

Caring for Someone Grieving

Losing a loved one is perhaps the most difficult thing a person can go through. In their time of sorrow, people who are grieving need to feel as if they are not alone. Though often the only thing you feel like you can do is just be there, here are some ways to actively support someone through the grieving process:

❀ Planning a memorial service can often be difficult. Ask family and friends at the funeral visitation if they would like to contribute to the service in some way.

❀ Encourage friends or family to stand up and tell a story about the deceased or to write their feelings down and send them to the family.

❀ Have someone tape the funeral service with a cassette player.

❀ Ask family and friends to bring photos of the deceased to the funeral to share with others.

❀ An alternative to a traditional funeral service is to wear colorful clothing to celebrate the life of the person who has passed on. Some people even choose to have balloons in celebration of the loved one's life.

❀ Help those coping with a loss to talk about their loved one. Begin the conversation for them by offering something special you remember.

❀ Help those who have lost someone special to start a cause that would be meaningful. For example, if the person died from an accident, the loved one might work for changes in legislation to provide safety measures to prevent similar accidents.

* At holidays or anniversary dates, include the memory of a loved one by getting out pictures, showing a video, or making that person's favorite dinner or dessert.

* Holidays are difficult after a loss. Send a card or note just to let the grieving person know you're thinking of him or her.

* On special occasions, buy a bouquet of daisies and take your grieving friend to the cemetery. Put your arm around your friend in comfort and silence.

* Call and ask if your grieving friend is ready to talk or wants company.

* Starting a journal is a private way to express feelings, so you might buy your friend a special book for writing in.

* Offer to house out-of-town relatives and friends who arrive for the memorial service.

* Funeral homes suggest asking someone to stay at the home (for security reasons) while everyone is at the service.

* The length of the grieving process differs for everyone. Continue to offer your support in some of the ways listed here for as long as needed.

Contentment in a Nursing Home

Marjorie was a schoolteacher who had enjoyed a long and happy marriage to her husband. When her husband died, Marjorie's friends helped her adjust to life as a widow. She attended many weekly church functions as well as various meetings and clubs. When Marjorie was eighty, she had knee surgery on both knees. Normally the doctors wouldn't perform surgery on someone her age, but because of her active lifestyle and good health, they went ahead. She recovered quickly and returned to her many activities in record time.

Marjorie was close to her ninetieth birthday when she suffered a slight stroke and spent many months in the hospital. Her only child lived thirty miles away, and they decided it would be difficult for her daughter to give Marjorie the constant care she needed. Also, Marjorie didn't want to impose on her daughter's busy lifestyle.

Marjorie's daughter started searching for a nursing home to accommodate her mother's needs. She found one that both she and her mother liked. While in the nursing home, Marjorie's mind remained sharp. The many friends who came to visit were always amazed at the books she read and the various projects she remained involved in.

Even though she liked the nursing home, Marjorie had difficulty adjusting to the isolation. In this particular nursing home, there were limited planned activities, and she missed preparing her own meals. She eased her loneliness by becoming close to the other residents. Evenings would find her pushing her walker up and down the halls, checking on each of her friends to be sure they were covered up, saying to each of them, "I don't want you to get cold." Finished with her evening task, she would return to her room and go to sleep, knowing that she was still needed.

❀ For a friend in a nursing home, find out what kinds of meals are served. If your friend likes special foods such as fresh fruit, check with the caregivers and see if you could bring some in.

❀ Inquire as to whether the residents have access to a television and VCR. If they do, ask what kind of movies they would enjoy. Libraries usually loan videotapes for a week, giving lots of time to view them.

❀ Nursing home residents can usually have their own bed, chair, and other personal items. Encourage people to keep as many personal possessions as possible with them.

❀ If they have photo albums in their rooms, plan time for a visit to look through them. If they make remarks about favorites, buy small frames and put those special photos in them.

❀ If they are able to get out for church or lunch, find out if they have regular plans to do so. If not, volunteer to set up a schedule so they can socialize outside the nursing home on a regular basis.

❁ If your friend uses a walker, consider buying one with big wheels and a basket on the front. When she or he goes out or even down the hall to the bathroom, the basket comes in handy to carry magazines, a scarf, or toiletries.

❁ Offer to sponsor a once-a-month bingo party. Bring prizes such as a deck of cards, book of crossword puzzles, brush, small plant, or picture frame. Invite the caregivers to join in the fun. This is an opportunity to take children along to volunteer.

❁ At holiday time, buy some cards and offer to address and stamp them for the residents. Let them write the message themselves, if possible.

❁ Plan a birthday party and take photos.

❁ Bring children to visit someone in a nursing home. Have them color a picture and leave it with the resident.

❁ Bring new sheets which are washed and ready-to-use for their bed.

❁ Make a date to take a nursing home resident for a drive and stop for an ice cream cone for the trip.

Caring for Someone in a Nursing Home

Moving into a nursing home and having to be dependent on others is difficult for everyone, especially those who are used to living on their own. Your support is needed as your loved one makes this transition. Help new residents realize that they are still loved and thought of by visiting and writing often. Show them that you still consider them a vital part of your life:

❀ Gather friends of all ages and visit a nursing home to sing carols during the holidays. Call ahead to arrange with the caregivers, and include them in the singing.

❀ Talk to the nursing home management and find out what kind of entertainment you could bring in for the residents, such as a card table with jigsaw puzzles for everyone to work on.

❀ Buy or rent books on tape, and take a small tape recorder to the nursing home.

❀ Arrange to take the patient on a regular basis to his or her own hair cutter or stylist.

❀ Seek out a counselor or minister to help the family through the transition of moving someone to a nursing home.

❀ Take as many treasured items as possible to the resident's room in the nursing home. Include framed pictures of relatives, a beloved afghan, even a favorite chair if it will fit.

❀ Purchase a "simple" music system for your loved one's

room, such as a combination radio and cassette player with built-in speakers. Bring the person's favorite music from home, and add a few new selections.

* When visiting, bring their favorite foods that aren't available in the nursing home. Perhaps they enjoy a certain flavor and brand of ice cream or crave chocolate-covered peanuts.

* Go for tea or coffee. Bring it hot in a thermos, and take your own china cups to serve it in. Pick up some fresh pastries on the way.

* Find out what games your loved one enjoys playing. Maybe he or she is a competitive Scrabble® player.

* Take family albums and go through them together. This can often help guide the conversation into some pleasantries about the past, and often you'll learn things you didn't know.

* Figure out what activities you can do in the group area of the nursing home. Explore the surrounding area as well. Are there picnic facilities available at a nearby lake? Is there a shopping mall that you can wheelchair your friend through just to people-watch?

* Select a new outfit for residents in their favorite colors. Get outfits that are attractive yet oversized, with elastic or large zippers for ease of dressing.

* If they are able to leave the nursing home, invite them to your home for a change of environment. If you are

visiting from out of town, arrange to have everyone spend the night at a local hotel.

❀ Pick your loved one up for lunch or dinner as often as you're able. While going out for dinner on a birthday or holiday is appreciated, spontaneous invitations are especially welcome.

❀ Try to find a nursing home that allows the patients to keep their pets with them.

❀ Take children over for brief visits. Having little ones around will bring out a smile.

❀ Bring a bowl of potpourri or fragrant flowers for their room.

❀ Bring a special or favorite dessert for the resident's dinner. Provide enough for everyone to share.

❀ Volunteer to read to someone in a nursing home.

❀ Arrange to take a friend of the resident to visit with him or her.

❀ A helpful book is *Nursing Homes: Getting Good Care There,* by Burger, Fraser, Hunt, and Frank.

Facing a Miscarriage

Ann and Jim had been married for six years when they decided they were ready to begin a family. About two months into the pregnancy, Ann began to bleed at home one weekend. She called the doctor's office and was told to rest and come in to the office on Monday. Jim was away for the weekend, so Ann began calling friends, wanting someone to console her. Her next-door neighbor picked up on the concern in Ann's voice. She knew that Ann might be miscarrying, but didn't want to say anything to her.

As the day went on, the bleeding and pain worsened. More concerned, Ann called her doctor again but was told to continue bed rest and come in on Monday. When Jim returned, he found Ann in pain, still bleeding and very concerned about what was happening to her. Ann was awake all night, too afraid to go to sleep. The pain was now coming in waves of contractions. She knew she was losing the baby.

On Monday morning the doctor sent them for an ultrasound, which showed nothing. They performed blood tests and were told it would take a day to get the results back. Ann found it very disconcerting that they couldn't confirm what she already knew had happened. On Tuesday, the doctor finally confirmed that they had lost the baby and scheduled a D & C procedure for later that afternoon.

Ann went home after the procedure and stared at the wall

in their bedroom. She didn't even know what to feel. They had not told anyone except their immediate family that they were expecting, so no one knew of their loss. She took the week off work and returned the following week only to face co-workers who wondered why she was gone. Not being able to share the loss made her feel even more isolated and sad.

Ann was well read on pregnancy and childbirth, but she had skipped over the sections on miscarriages. Now she felt very uninformed and wanted to know everything. Why did this happen? What if they tried again and lost a second baby? She began to talk about it with close friends and learned that many women experience miscarriages. She even found out that her own mother had suffered four miscarriages, which she had never known about.

Ann's close friend had a two-month-old baby. Ann called her and asked if she could come over for a visit. She was overpowered with strong feelings of needing to hold a baby. As she held the tiny infant, tears fell onto the soft sleeper. Now she better understood her loss, for she couldn't describe how wonderful it was to hold a baby. She knew they would try again. Several years later, Ann and Jim were overjoyed when they gave birth to their first son.

❀ Give parents who have experienced a miscarriage a journal to write their feelings in.

❀ Encourage them to discuss their loss with others

through support groups.

- ❀ Bring over a hot meal for people grieving a miscarriage.
- ❀ Purchase a gift certificate at a hotel or bed and breakfast inn for a change of scenery and a chance for reflection.
- ❀ Allow those who have experienced a miscarriage to grieve the loss in their own way and time.
- ❀ The loss of an unborn child can be just as difficult as the loss of a full-term baby. Give the would-be parents a stuffed animal, which could provide comfort as well as become a keepsake for recording the memory.
- ❀ Respect the privacy of those who experience miscarriage, and give them time to work through this together.
- ❀ Help with physical chores such as laundry, cooking, or shopping.
- ❀ Gather co-workers to assist in helping with their projects at work.
- ❀ Have a memorial service at a local church for family members to mourn the loss, if this feels appropriate to them.

Caring After a Loss

Here are more ideas for supporting someone who has lost a loved one:

❀ People handle loss in their own way, whether it is the loss of a loved one, a job, or one's health. If we can reach out in any way to support a person who has faced a loss, we can help them overcome their grief. During the weeks and months after the funeral or layoff, support is really appreciated.

❀ If parents have lost children, take them to a Compassionate Friends Support Group meeting. This group is made up of parents who have all lost children. Sometimes in order to heal, it is necessary to connect with others who share your type of loss.

❀ Offer to take your friend out for something you can both enjoy on a regular basis, such as a movie, golfing, or a cup of coffee.

❀ Be sensitive to the holidays for people who are grieving. A "happy holiday" card may not seem appropriate, but a card or a letter of encouragement just to let them know you are thinking about them would be appreciated.

❀ Discuss their holiday plans, and include them in yours if possible.

❀ Be patient with those mourning a loss. Suggest they communicate their feelings with a friend or counselor.

❀ Go visit friends who are grieving and just give them a

big hug; no other communication is needed.

❀ If you know someone who needs additional help coping with the loss, make an appointment with a medical professional. If possible, go with your friend to the first visit.

❀ Check with funeral homes, the local health department, and counseling centers for upcoming seminars on grief, which usually are offered throughout the year.

❀ Help those dealing with a loss to talk about their loved one. Ask them what the deceased's favorite food or hobby was. Allow them time to tell you stories about their loved one. If they begin to cry, don't stop the process, but encourage it.

❀ Offer a shoulder to cry on for as long as your friend needs it. There is no timetable in which we "get over" our grief. We all grieve in different ways and for different periods of time.

❀ Acknowledge the anniversary by sending a gift, flowers, or a card.

❀ If you too have gone through a loss, describe your experience in a letter to someone who is grieving. This is empathy at its best.

❀ Provide books, videos, or crossword puzzles.

Starting Again

Sarah was having trouble making a new life for herself. Her children had been gone for several years now, living their own lives in different parts of the country. With the recent death of her husband, she was at a loss about how to fill her time. The group of friends she used to do things with when her husband was alive just wasn't the same anymore. Over time, she slowly dropped out of these social activities.

She began to look around her big house, which she and her husband had built for their retirement. She felt depressed being there all alone. Part of her knew she should move on and find a new place more suited to her new lifestyle. Yet part of her knew how difficult that move would be. She had grown accustomed to her life as it was. The thought of leaving was very unsettling. A younger Sarah would not have wavered over these decisions.

Sarah found it difficult to get up in the morning. She knew she needed to be around other people, and she especially missed her family. So a few weeks later she flew to Arizona to visit her daughter. While there, she realized how much she missed warm weather. She loved being able to go out for daily walks. The night before she was to leave, her daughter suggested that she move there.

Sarah returned several weeks later and began looking for a place to live. She found a small town about twenty miles from her daughter, which seemed perfect for her. She bought a condominium and prepared to move. She knew she had many productive days left and was ready to start a new chapter in her life. Because her daughter worked full-time, Sarah was able to take care of her grandchildren on a regular basis. Sarah enjoyed their school activities and became very involved with the school, even volunteering one day per week there. Sarah found the involvement with her grandchildren more fulfilling than she had ever imagined.

❀ When someone is moving across the country, arrange for family or friends to be there as the moving van arrives.

❀ At the new home, help put the beds together, and put the essential kitchen items away so your loved one can feel settled.

❀ Inquire on behalf of your new resident friend about social groups available in your area. There is usually a listing in the community resource department or in the local paper.

❀ Go with a new resident to open a bank account. Many senior citizens are overwhelmed by the many options offered by banks.

❀ Purchase a local map and highlight key areas, such as grocery stores, the library, and movie theaters. Take new residents on a driving tour.

- ❀ Ask whether they would like a pet to keep them company. If they are not up for the responsibility of caring for one, suggest they volunteer at the Humane Society as a way to be around animals without the long-term commitment.

- ❀ Introduce them to an athletic club or local YMCA. These clubs usually have great classes for seniors where they can make new friends while staying in good physical shape.

- ❀ Provide a listing of volunteer needs within the community. Most communities have staff members who can fit you with the right agency, depending on your skills and the amount of time you want to be involved.

- ❀ Suggest new residents volunteer at a local school. Teachers are always grateful for an extra pair of hands to help with school projects.

- ❀ If you know senior citizens who like to drive and have time on their hands, suggest they run errands for others who can't.

- ❀ Arrange for a friend or relative to come visit.

- ❀ Purchase new home announcement cards and stamps for someone who has moved.

Caring for Someone Who Is Lonely

More than anything else, lonely people need to be reminded that they are not truly alone. A lonely person needs very personal and individual attention. Let a lonely friend know you are thinking about him or her specifically and that you care about your friend's welfare. Here are some ways to brighten up a lonely person's day:

* Organize a letter-writing campaign. Assign friends and relatives to send a note on a certain day each week so the person will receive mail almost daily.

* Send someone a box of gifts for the week. Wrap seven items such as pictures your children have made, a magazine, an envelope of hot chocolate, gum, or candy. Send a note telling the person to open one per day.

* Take a stuffed animal to someone lonely.

* Give the person a bowl with one or two goldfish.

* If you know a lonely senior citizen who could use companionship, help that person find a support group or hobby. Attend the first meeting with that person.

* Have a child record a story, sing a song, or recite a poem on a cassette tape and give to a lonely friend.

* For someone who can't get out regularly, make video-tapes for them. Tape your children, the outdoors, someplace you've visited. Make this fun!

* Organize a progressive dinner once a month for a group of lonely people.

- ❀ Arrange a surprise visit from a special friend or relative for someone who is lonely.

- ❀ Plan an annual birthday party. Take photographs and put them in an album for a friend to keep.

- ❀ When you stop to visit someone lonely, stay long enough to let the person talk. Lonely people miss talking to others.

- ❀ Help your friend get involved with children. Day care centers and preschools always need an extra set of loving hands.

- ❀ Get up early and pick up someone who is lonely. Find a quiet spot to watch the sun come up and share a thermos of coffee.

- ❀ Remember during the holidays to involve children and senior citizens in local community activities, such as helping serve a Thanksgiving meal to the needy or filling holiday baskets at a local church.

- ❀ When you shop for a card for someone lonely, you may find three or four that are cheery. Buy them all and send them on the same day. Besides the warm words, your friend will have the thrill of having their mailbox overflow!

- ❀ Take someone lonely to a travel series through the local community education program. These inspire people to travel to new destinations.

The Kindness of Strangers

David, a Presbyterian minister, was transferred to a church position in Minnesota in July. That year, Christmas Day began as it does for many families, with the early morning awakening and gathering around the tree to open gifts. David had gotten up early to clean out the fireplace so they could build a fire on Christmas Day. After putting the ashes in the trash container in the garage, he returned to their living room to open gifts. Soon the family smelled smoke, and when they ran to the garage, they were amazed to see a fire started. David and his family ran to their neighbors and called the fire department. While the firefighters fought to put out the fire, David and Betty could not even look at their home burning. Another minister picked up David and his family and took them to their home to spend Christmas Day.

David was especially upset when he saw his cars hauled out of the garage in ruins. They began taking an inventory of everything that was damaged. Using a cassette recorder they walked through each room in their minds and tried to recreate their lost items.

A minister from another church offered him the use of his house for a week. A third church found a mobile home David and Betty and their son could use until theirs was rebuilt. A fourth church in the area donated furniture, a television, and other household items for them to use. They stayed in this temporary home for five months. They were grateful that the temporary home was close to their son's school so he could still see his best friend on a daily basis.

When David and Betty returned to their home several days after the fire, they found a pot where a small stalk of a spider plant had survived. They still have the plant, which reminds them of how blessed they are to be alive.

- ❀ If you take in people who have faced a disaster, allow them time and space to deal with their grief and shock. Provide food and shelter, but give them space to be alone.
- ❀ Bring in meals and offer to do grocery shopping for the family for at least the first week.
- ❀ If you are a relative who lives far away, send money and/ or gift certificates for the items that people whose home has been destroyed need to replace.
- ❀ If you have photos of the family members, get reprints or enlargements made and send to them. Give the family a photo album, camera, and film so they can begin to take new photos.
- ❀ Help the children to keep their schedule as normal as possible, such as the same school, friends, and after-school activities.
- ❀ If you know a plumber, contractor, electrician, or painter, offer to contact them.

- ❋ Offer to help with the cleanup—which is needed after most natural disasters.
- ❋ If the fire, flood, or tornado damaged their yard, offer to have a landscaping business replace bushes, trees, or grass.
- ❋ Buy new house numbers or a decorative mailbox when the repairs are done and they are moving back into their home.
- ❋ Arrange a surprise party of neighbors, friends, or relatives when the family is able to move back into their home.
- ❋ Purchase a mini-cassette recorder for the family to record items that need replacing.
- ❋ Give the family general merchandise gift certificates.
- ❋ Replace a cookbook, a calendar, and an address book.

CHAPTER FOUR

Relationships

It's hard for any of us to imagine our lives without the relationships with our family and friends. We discover who we are by learning about and growing with the people who touch our lives. Though relationships are sometimes difficult, we expand our understanding of ourselves by opening our hearts and minds to others.

Maintaining all relationships takes commitment and creativity. Consistency of care and love becomes key in developing lasting and meaningful relationships. We need to let the people we love know we care about them regularly. Such things cannot be taken for granted, because we need consistent and reliable love just as much as we need food and water. This chapter explores the power of relationship in all forms and will help you acknowledge and continue your commitment to the people you hold dear.

"And what is as important as knowledge?"
asked the mind.
"Caring and seeing with the heart,"
answered the soul.

ANONYMOUS

Coping with Teenage Turmoil

The door slammed. The music started again at its normal high volume. Jean sighed, knowing her daughter would be in her room for the night and any further attempt at communication would be futile. Since her daughter's new morning routine was to stay in her room until she heard her parents leave for work, there would be no chance to talk then, either.

Jean was confused by the changes in her daughter Jessica's behavior and demeanor. She knew from talking with other parents that teenagers could be difficult and challenging. She tried to recall her own teenage years but was unable to remember anything like what she and her daughter were going through. Until a few months ago, she had enjoyed a special relationship with Jessica. In the last several years, their almost-every-weekend shopping trips had kept them close. With both of them wearing the same size, they often found themselves "fighting" over a sweater they both liked. Knowing how close they had been, Jean now felt confused about what had changed so abruptly.

Jean had prided herself on being a mother who was always there, not only for Jessica, but for her friends as well. She was agreeable to most of the social activities Jessica proposed. Jean usually volunteered to drive Jessica and her friends, because she enjoyed their company and was happy that they still enjoyed hers.

But all of that had stopped, and the person who now resided in Jessica's bedroom was a stranger to the family. Jessica started receiving phone calls from friends her mother had never heard of. Even Jessica's style of clothes changed drastically. She no longer informed her mother of school functions and activities. Jean wondered if this change was from overprotective parenting. Did Jessica need to experience her freedom?

Jean continued to show Jessica that she trusted her and hoped that her change in behavior would be short-lived. However, Jean's concern deepened when one morning she took out the trash and discovered liquor bottles, which could have come only from Jessica. Gripping the bag intensely, Jean did not know what to do next.

❁ Assist parents of teens in forming their own support group with their children's friend's parents and possibly teachers who are concerned.

❁ Take your friend out to lunch, and listen to the problems she or he is having with a teenager.

❁ Send your friend a card with the message that "this too shall pass."

❁ Clip magazine articles related to teenagers and their problems.

❁ Suggest an outing that your friend and his or her teenager could attend to try to reconnect, such as a shopping trip to another city or a sporting event.

- ❀ Give brochures and travel information for an outing.
- ❀ Suggest your friend write a letter to the teenager when she or he is frustrated about not being able to communicate. When the time is appropriate, give the letter to the teenager. Sometimes it takes written communication to break down the barriers.
- ❀ Send the teenager a note or card every week just to show you are thinking about him or her and that you care.
- ❀ Take the teen out once a week for dessert and conversation.
- ❀ Encourage the teen's grandparents to spend time with her or him. They will sometimes give a different perspective on the situation.
- ❀ Encourage the teen to keep a diary.
- ❀ Suggest to the teen to talk to a school counselor.
- ❀ Give parents of a teenager *Wonderful Ways to Love a Teen, Even When It Seems Impossible,* by Judy Ford.

Caring Celebrations

Coming up with a new and different way to celebrate your loved one's birthday every year can be a test of the imagination. The important thing to remember is that the day becomes special through your act of caring, no matter what it is. Here are some ideas to help you plan the big day:

- ❀ Every birthday is a wonderful celebration of life. Make the day fun!

- ❀ Make a donation to the birthday person's favorite charity.

- ❀ Throw a party, and in lieu of gifts ask everyone to write a few thoughts about the birthday person. Have a decorative box or bag to put all the notes in. Could you imagine receiving lots of kind and loving letters from your closest friends?

- ❀ Be sensitive to people's feelings about parties (especially surprise parties), and find out first if they would enjoy this.

- ❀ If you are planning a party, be sure to invite out-of-town friends and relatives. They may not attend, but they will appreciate being invited so they can send a gift or card.

- ❀ Ask friends and relatives to bring a photo of them with the birthday person to the party.

- ❀ Assign someone attending the party to take a photo of

each person with the guest of honor, and then put them all in a photo album for him or her.

❀ If you know someone special who could not attend the party, ask that person to call while the party is in full swing.

❀ For those who cannot attend, ask them to send a message on cassette or videotape for the birthday person.

❀ Check with co-workers, and find out if and how they would like to celebrate their birthday at the office. Many enjoy a cake and singing, but others would rather have their birthdays be very low key.

❀ Have a party for the birthday person's pet, and invite friends. Gifts could be pet food or a contribution to the Humane Society.

❀ Plan a surprise birthday party for a minister, rabbi, or priest after the service. Bring a cake, and have the congregation sign a banner.

❀ When planning a party, make a collage of photos from the birthday person's life. This gives the attendees something to talk about to break the ice.

Caring on a Special Day

Here are some more fun ways to celebrate a birthday:

❀ Send someone the number of cards corresponding to his or her age. For example, send sixteen cards to someone celebrating a sixteenth birthday.

❀ Send the number of balloons corresponding to the birthday person's age.

❀ Give new one-dollar bills for each year of age. Children love this one.

❀ For a creative gift, have everyone contribute toward an airline ticket to the destination of a place the birthday person has always wanted to go.

❀ Mail the number of cards of the birthday person's age, one per day, prior to the birthday. For someone turning thirty, mail one card each day for a month before the birthday.

❀ Give the dollar amount of the person's age in gift certificates for movies, a restaurant, or a bookstore.

❀ For someone with a particular interest or hobby, tailor your gift to that hobby. For instance, an antique lover will enjoy a stay at a bed-and-breakfast inn.

❀ Plan a party and invite the number of guests relevant to the person's age, such as fifty guests for someone turning fifty.

❀ If your loved one has a passion for a particular candy,

purchase the number of pieces equal to her or his age. Give forty candy bars to someone turning forty.

❀ Donate a book to the library in honor of someone's birthday.

❀ Make a homemade coupon book with certificates for dinner, backrub, or breakfast in bed.

❀ Send the person celebrating a birthday the number of flowers of his or her age, such as twenty-one roses or carnations for someone turning twenty-one.

❀ Throw a birthday party in which everyone brings items to donate to the local food bank.

❀ Each year, have the birthday person hold a sign with her or his age on it. Then take your friend's picture. Give your friend a special album to keep the photos in year after year.

❀ Have a cake or special dessert delivered to the birthday person at work.

❀ Give the birthday person several envelopes on their birthday, each containing a gift certificate. One could be for lunch, one for their favorite store, one for flowers, one for dinner and a movie.

Caring Enough to Give the Right Gift

The most important thing to remember when giving a gift is who you are giving it to. Think of your loved one's needs and wants as you are choosing a gift. You know the person well, so make sure you use what you know to help you in your choice. Give because you want to, as often and whatever you want. Do it because it makes you feel good. Following are some gift ideas you might not have considered that could be perfect for your loved one:

❀ Purchasing an item that you heard a loved one ask for will always be more special than an expensive gift that was unrequested. The perfect birthday gift might be those special cream puffs that you know your friend occasionally treats himself or herself to.

❀ For graduation, give students gift certificates to a bookstore, sporting gear store, favorite restaurant or theater. This becomes more memorable than just giving money.

❀ College students really appreciate gift certificates to general merchandise stores.

❀ For those people who have everything (like your parents), consider giving them the gift of a visit if you don't get to see them very often. If your mom likes to shop, schedule a shopping weekend for her and all of your sisters for her birthday, leaving spouses and children behind. If your dad enjoys golf, arrange for breakfast and eighteen holes, followed by lunch with the entire family. Plan a weekend at a resort for the whole family.

❀ For people who can't get out, purchase the latest videos or pick up a bestselling book.

❀ For people who live alone, always purchase tickets in pairs so that they can take a friend.

❀ Buy a jigsaw puzzle for someone who lives alone. Once the pieces are out on a card table, they will be drawn to finish it, whether they are a puzzle lover or not. Even visitors to their home will find themselves searching to make a match.

❀ Purchase restaurant gift certificates for a friend who likes to go out for breakfast on the way to work. On the gift certificate, tape change for buying his or her favorite newspaper.

❀ Help your friend's children to make homemade Mother's Day or Father's Day gifts—a handmade card accompanied by chocolate chip muffins.

❀ Get the gift they would never buy for themselves. Many people wouldn't buy expensive gourmet coffee but would praise the giver as they savored each cup.

❀ Send a basket with a new pen set, coffee mug, or mousepad for your friend starting a new job.

❀ Give the stay-at-home mom special cookie sheets shaped in the form of gingerbread children. Include all of the ingredients for her and her children to have an afternoon activity of baking cookies.

❀ Send surprise packages, like a big tin of popcorn to a friend who is a popcorn fan.

❀ Send gifts to your friend's place of employment. Ask a florist for something unique, like an arrangement of delicate little flowers in an old teacup with a saucer.

❀ Know what your friend collects, such as antique kitchen items, then when you see something, pick it up to add to their collection.

❀ Don't save gift giving for holidays. Be spontaneous throughout the year by leaving a little wrapped candy bar, a card, or a stuffed animal, particularly for those who are close friends and family members.

❀ When shopping with a friend, keep an eye out for an item he or she looks at twice. Go back later, buy it, and save it for a special occasion.

❀ If you know someone who wants to return to college, give a gift certificate to cover some tuition or text-books.

❀ Give children items to start a collection, like teddy bears, snow globes, coins, or stamps.

❀ At holiday time, give a new ornament each year to add to a special collection.

❀ For teens who participate in a sport, get them a charm or sweatshirt with a symbol of their sport on it.

Caring Gifts Are Always Welcome

Just because you are late with a gift does not mean you don't care. Still take the time to make sure you are giving a kind and meaningful gift. Your loved one might actually appreciate your lengthening their celebration by giving a late gift:

- ❀ Late baby gifts are *always* welcome and often more appreciated, as the baby has outgrown infant outfits and toys received earlier.
- ❀ If you received high school graduation announcements yet somehow never got around to responding, surprise the graduate entering college that fall with a card and every college student's favorite: cash!
- ❀ A forgotten birthday just gives you the chance to be more creative. You can fill a letter with all kinds of creative excuses as to why you forgot.
- ❀ Children usually receive so many gifts at once that they can't fully appreciate them. Make it one of your special traditions with them to be perpetually late with your gift, just to elongate the memory for them.
- ❀ Holiday gifts that didn't quite make it can be given as New Year's gifts.
- ❀ If you didn't get a card in the mail on time, call and leave a message on the person's answering machine. Sing a little tune for an extra special message.
- ❀ Send a belated greeting card.

Transition to College

For weeks Shelly had been sorting through items, going back and forth about what to pack for college. Spread out in her bedroom were new clothes as well as old, familiar things. Shelly packed her favorite slippers and the afghan her mother had made years ago. She gathered up her yearbooks from high school; she still wanted to feel close to her friends. Her mother had taken her shopping for a few room decorations, but they decided it was best to wait and see what her roommate would bring. Shelly hoped that she had been paired with someone compatible.

Shelly had visited the college orientation two days during the summer and had been overwhelmed with the size of the campus. She wondered how she would ever find her classes. Shelly would be starting a pre-med curriculum and had been informed by others that the classes were difficult. They also told her that many students didn't make it through the first year.

She knew she had to be strong while dealing with the emotions of leaving her home, family, and friends. Her parents took her to college the first day, and when she arrived at the dorm, her roommate was not there yet. She was not sure what to do next, so she just set her things down. Her parents took her to lunch. They tried to keep the conversation light, as they all knew good-byes were coming soon. Shelly's parents walked her back to her dorm, hugged her, and kissed her good-bye.

She noticed they had tears in their eyes. Fighting off her own tears, she held her head up, turned, and waved, returning to her room to begin a new chapter in life.

❀ Students who live in a dorm often have most but not all meals provided. Find out what day and meals the students are on their own, and then give gift certificates they can use at those times.

❀ An eagerly anticipated event at all dormitories is the daily mailbox check. Anyone receiving mail is sure to walk away with a big smile.

❀ The best care packages are the ones that come with something homemade, maybe a childhood favorite. Send a tightly sealed box of chocolate chip cookies, krispie treats, or brownies.

❀ If you have a voice-mail system at work, see if your student can be added to one of the guest boxes so that he or she can leave and receive messages from you.

❀ At holiday time, send a care package that includes holiday decorations for the student's room.

❀ For the freshman's first report card, send a note of congratulations, a bouquet of flowers, or a telegram congratulating the student on getting through the first term at school.

❀ Help students find personal items to make their room more "homey." A popcorn popper, microwave, refrigerator, rocking chair, or beanbag chair are suggestions.

- Buy tokens or passes to give the student for transportation as well as to shop or go out for meals and entertainment.

- When visiting your college student, stop by a grocery store and stock up on beverages and snacks.

- Students' addresses change frequently, so help develop a change-of-address letter along with preprinted labels to send to friends and family.

- If your child is a sports fan, buy season passes for his or her favorite college sport such as football, tennis, or basketball.

- On one of your first visits to the college, visit the local bookstore and pick up T-shirts, sweatshirts, and hats with the school colors and logo so that you can show your support.

- Extra spending cash is always needed, wanted, and appreciated.

- Mark the tough weeks, like exam weeks, on your calendar. Since these are frequently weeks where students don't get enough sleep, don't eat right, and are stressed for study time, send messages of encouragement. This could mean sending a pizza and soda to their dorm room some evening, sending a note of encouragement each day of the week, or mailing a big box of miniature candy bars.

Caring Through Correspondence

We all know how hard it sometimes is to keep in touch with people we don't see every day. As much as we care about our distant friends and relatives, it's often difficult to show them we are thinking about them. Here are some fun and unusual ways to keep in touch:

* Send letters to college students filled with thoughts and updates about what is going on at home.

* Buy stationery you like and stamps to match. Find time to write at least one letter per week.

* Keep cards and stationery in your desk at work.

* Purchase small note cards or postcards, and keep them in your purse. You'll be able to jot a few lines to someone while you are waiting for an appointment or having lunch.

* Send flowers once a month to a favorite person. You can set this up with a florist to deliver them each month on the same day.

* Keep a calendar with special occasions such as birthdays, and check it at the beginning of each week.

* When you have time, browse the card shop and select several different cards so they will be ready to send.

* Purchase a selection of sympathy cards, and have them available to send when you hear of someone's loss.

* Send cards or letters to children of all ages on a regular basis. They rarely receive mail and love to have some-

thing come that is just for them.

❀ For friends who are moving, give them stationery and stamped envelopes with your address on them to encourage them to keep in touch with you.

❀ If loved ones have just moved, send a card so that they will have instant mail from someone they know.

❀ Senior citizens love to hear how and what their friends and relatives are doing. Send a card, or call on a regular basis.

❀ If a family member is having a difficult time, send a letter to other family members asking them to support the person.

❀ If you have a good friend you want to keep in touch with but just never seem to be able to, write on your calendar to call or write the person on a certain day. You will soon find you are keeping in touch quite regularly.

❀ Be sure to keep in touch with teenagers. Write to them, and include memories of things you recall they did as a child. If you knew their parents when they were teenagers, share experiences about what their parents did when they were the teen's age.

❀ Send photos to children of themselves or family members.

❀ Take videos or photos at all get togethers of family or friends, and send them to the members who could not make the event.

* Be the person to plan and host a family reunion or holiday gathering.

* Start a twice-a-year family chain letter. Write about what's going on with your family, then pass it on to the next relative to add to it, to pass to the next family. Then the final family can return it to you.

* Consider having all family members get an e-mail address for ease of communications.

* Some people find that sending a letter to a friend or loved one helps them to connect. Write your dreams down and send them to a friend.

* For someone who is facing a challenge, send a letter of hope and encouragement.

* Think of a friend or loved one who has enriched your life and send them a thank you letter.

Moving On . . . After Divorce

When John and Sue married, they began their relationship by talking for hours about their dreams and desires. Their relationship seemed to change after the birth of their daughter. John became absorbed with his job, and there just didn't seem to be time to talk to each other. Sue had given up her full-time job to care for the baby, and while she enjoyed being a mother, she at times felt lonely. The days all seemed the same: taking care of the baby, laundry, meals, and cleaning. She yearned for time to talk with John. She tried to suggest times they could get together, but that didn't seem to work. She suggested that once a week he come home for lunch, but that only happened once. When Sue's birthday came and John arrived home empty-handed, his response was, "I know it is your birthday, but I was too busy to buy you anything." At this point in their marriage, Sue insisted they try marriage counseling. Sue read all the latest psychology and relationship books she could find at the library. She encouraged John to read them also, but again, he was too busy with work.

Sue contemplated divorce on many occasions but tended to blame herself for their lack of communication, thinking maybe she should try harder or maybe she didn't really understand his pressures at work. Sue even suggested to John that he develop some friendships or pursue a hobby, but the response always was, "I'm too busy at work."

Even though they continued to live in the same house, Sue and John didn't share meals or social activities. They didn't even discuss their day with each other. After some years, Sue resolved to go forward with the divorce. But the decision was so painful that she needed a great deal of support and encouragement from family members and friends.

❀ Make an appointment with a lawyer for an hour of consultation for your friend. The first step in divorce proceedings can be the hardest. Offer to accompany your friend to the lawyer's office.

❀ Treat your friend to a haircut with a gift certificate from her or his favorite salon.

❀ Be available when a newly separated friend needs to talk about his or her feelings.

❀ Remember your friend on Valentine's Day with a gift or card.

❀ Offer to assist on tough days such as court appearances. Get together with your friend for the three c's: coffee, conversation, and chocolate!

❀ If you have time, schedule a walk with your friend on a regular basis, or take an exercise class together.

❀ Ask about holiday plans, for they definitely will be different now for your friend.

❀ Send coping or encouragement cards once a week, or write your own words in a letter. Your words can be especially important if you have experienced divorce yourself.

❀ Rent *Sleepless in Seattle* and watch it together. Better yet, buy your friend a copy.

❀ Give your friend a catalog of classes at the local community college. If possible, take a class with him or her.

❀ When the divorce is final, go with your friend to court. Take your friend out afterward to celebrate a new beginning.

❀ If you have mutual friends, check with one another frequently to see how your newly divorced friend is coping.

❀ Give the children of divorce age-appropriate books on the subject, such as *My Parents Are Divorced, Too,* by Jan Blackstone-Ford.

❀ Encourage extended family members to give extra attention to the children at the time of separation.

❀ Give a copy of *The Good Divorce,* by Constance R. Ahrons, Ph.D.

Bonding as a New Family

Elaine and Mark, both divorced, met through a mutual friend. Upon discovering so many common interests, they began dating. At the time, Elaine's children were six and nine. Mark also had two children, seven and eight. Elaine and Mark's early dates consisted of spending time together on the weekends when their children were with their exspouses. After a few months, the children met and, at first, were happy about having new playmates.

Elaine and Mark's relationship grew to the point where they both wanted to make it permanent. When the children found out that Elaine and Mark were getting married, they were far from overjoyed. Anxious questions surfaced: Was this a new mom or dad, and what about their other mom and dad? Would they still see their other parents? Where would they live, and who would be in which room? Elaine and Mark assured them that everything would work out. Eventually the children got excited about the wedding, especially since Mark and Elaine had a special role for each of them in the ceremony.

The night of the wedding, when Mark and Elaine were away spending their first night as a married couple, the kids became nervous. Elaine's children realized that their mother now had someone, other than them, who was very important to her. Because they had moved to Mark's house, Elaine's children were having to change homes and schools, and neither of them was happy about it.

As the year progressed, they worked through many typical blended family issues. Everyone eventually got her or his own room, which seemed to ease some of the sibling rivalry. They started new holiday traditions. Elaine and Mark decided it would be nice to have another child, but they wondered what impact that would have on the family. To their surprise, the children seemed overjoyed when they made the announcement. Andrew was born about one year after Elaine and Mark married. His arrival helped the family take another step in blending their lives together.

※ Give grandparents and relatives current pictures of your stepchildren. Try to obtain copies of them as young children or babies.

※ Keep in the kids' rooms pictures of all the children with you and with their biological mom or dad.

※ Encourage relatives to talk to all the children when they call, not just to their blood grandchildren.

※ As parents, try to spend time with each child individually on a regular basis, such as taking one out to breakfast, taking another to a sports event, going shopping with another.

※ Parents need to schedule a monthly date with each other, so they have time away from the children to discuss problems and concerns.

* When becoming a blended family, have everyone participate in decisions such as bedrooms and chores. Start out making everyone feel she or he is entitled to have opinions and make suggestions.

* If children seem to be having problems at school, enlist the counselor to talk with the student and/or the parents. Becoming a blended family is a major life change and causes a great deal of stress for most children.

* Fill new photo albums with pictures of the blended family, and let everyone have a turn taking the pictures.

* Post a list of chores and daily activities, and be sure that everyone has some responsibility. This makes children feel needed.

* Have children help with making their favorite dinner once a week.

* Recognize that holidays will be different in a new family. Before each holiday, discuss rituals that either family may have had, then decide on which ones to keep or which new ones to follow.

* Host a new family shower. Gifts could include certificates for family outings, such as sporting events, circus tickets, and movie passes.

* Take a gift for the whole family, such as a picnic basket or camping supplies.

Caring Before and After a Move

Packing up and moving a family is more than just a physical hassle. It takes an emotional toll on people to leave a place they are familiar with and to move to a new home they don't yet feel comfortable in. Help your loved ones make this transition by offering both physical and emotional support. Assist in the actual moving process, but also be sure to acknowledge their emotional needs. Here are some ideas for helping loved ones and new neighbors begin to feel at home in their new home:

❀ Revive the old tradition of taking some freshly baked cookies, a dish of food, or other homemade item to a new neighbor.

❀ Give a subscription to a local city events magazine to someone who is new to the area.

❀ If you are the handy type, offer to help hang pictures, put up light fixtures, or do other odd jobs.

❀ For someone moving, buy gift certificates to hardware or general merchandise stores. Setting up a household is always more expensive than expected.

❀ Arrange a housecleaning service for cleaning up their old house or preparing the new one.

❀ If friends you know have moved to your area, help them learn to know their way around by taking them on a tour and showing them places they need to go, such as banks, grocery stores, and gas stations.

❀ Help someone get established by making a list of doctors, dentists, and other health practitioners. Offer to call and see if these offices are accepting new patients.

❀ If a new family in town has children, offer to take them while the parents go out; they won't know who to ask to baby-sit yet.

❀ Prepare a recommended list of baby-sitters with their names and addresses.

❀ Assist new parents in town find extracurricular activities for their children. Put together a list of music teachers or coaches to help get the children involved.

❀ Pick up change-of-address cards from the post office so friends who are moving can send them to magazine offices, insurance companies, or banks.

❀ Purchase "new home" announcement cards, and offer to address them to their family and friends. Take a picture of the family in front of their new home holding a sign with their address and phone number. You could use this as the announcement card.

❀ Offer to go along while your friend is house hunting. Take notes on what she or he liked at each visit.

❀ On a friend's moving day, bring over a pot of chili, cookies, and soft drinks for the day. A pot of coffee and doughnuts would be welcome in the morning.

The Importance of Grandparents

Bob and Carol adored their grandchildren. They made every effort to celebrate their birthdays and attend school activities. Bob and Carol had looked forward to retirement so that they could spend more time with their grandchildren. Then, in a moment, their dream was shattered. Their daughter was killed in a car accident. Their son-in-law could not cope with the tragedy, so he took the children and moved to another state. Losing their daughter was unbearable, but not being able to see their grandchildren made it worse. They wondered how to keep in touch with the grandchildren now that they could no longer see them in person.

Mary and Ted cherished similar dreams of spending time with their grandchildren. The years ahead were to be filled with family reunions, picnics, and taking their grandchildren on summer vacations with them. One spring they purchased a mobile home and eagerly stocked it with snacks. They spent many evenings by the fire mapping out their July trip. Then their son called one day to tell them that he and his wife were divorcing. This put an end to the summer vacation plans, because now the grandchildren would be split between parents for holidays and summer recess. Mary and Ted were at a loss as to how to stay connected to their grandchildren.

David and Ruth's story has a happier ending. They had spent their lives as busy medical professionals and now were happy to be retired. They took time to plan vacations with their grandchildren. They called weekly and talked to the children, sent e-mail, and never doubted they had a place in the children's lives. The time they spent with their grandchildren was special and added a deeper meaning to their retirement years. But they wondered what else they might do to deepen their relationship with the grandchildren.

When Sally's husband died, she moved across the country to live close to her son and his family. She found that being involved in her grandchildren's lives gave her a reason to get up every day. She kept her three-year-old grandson three afternoons a week, which filled those empty days. Every Friday, she volunteered at the children's school. The school grew to depend on her being there, and she was pleased to feel needed again. The little hugs and kisses made her day!

Though everyone's story is different, grandparents share the need to be a part of their grandchildren's lives. Here are some suggestions for staying in touch with grandchildren:

- Grandparents can pass on their family history by writing their stories in a journal or recording it on tape.
- Grandparents need to take the time to tell their grandchildren about when they were young and especially what the children's parents were like as children.
- Record yourself reading a book (maybe for the grandchild's birthday), and send it to the child.

❀ If you are grandparents of stepgrandchildren, take the time to get to know each child individually. Take pictures of them often, and add them to your family albums. Ask for pictures of them as young children to add to the album.

❀ Some grandparents have difficulty accepting interracial marriages or grandchildren who have been adopted. Sit down as a family and find ways to overcome the barriers and decide how best to get to know one another.

❀ Plan vacations for you and your grandchildren. This could be a week's vacation to another part of the country or an evening at a local hotel with swimming, playing games, and just being together.

❀ Going on a cruise may be appropriate for some families, or you might prefer to take your grandchildren strawberry picking in the summer and teach them to make shortcake. In the fall, consider picking apples or pumpkins.

❀ If you plan activities that you enjoy doing, chances are your grandchildren will pick up your enthusiasm.

❀ Ask your grandchildren about school and their friends.

❀ Offer to take your grandchild for a haircut, dentist, or doctor appointment.

❀ If you volunteer your time in the community, ask your grandchild to accompany you.

❀ Call and ask just to speak with your grandchild, not as

an afterthought after talking with Mom or Dad.

- ❀ Give the grandchild a family heirloom such as a ring, watch, or books.
- ❀ Take the time to play board and card games with grandchildren.
- ❀ Help grandchildren begin a collection such as coins, stamps, or sports cards. Add to their collection on special occasions such as birthdays.
- ❀ Plan a monthly date with each grandchild.
- ❀ Have your grandchildren teach you computer skills.
- ❀ Attend your grandchildren's school functions.
- ❀ Teach your grandchildren a hobby you enjoy or learn a new one together.
- ❀ Plan a summer vacation with grandparents, parents, and the children.

Caring Across the Miles

Here are some more interesting ways to let distant friends or relatives know you are thinking about them:

❀ When visiting a relative or friend on an infrequent basis, make some traditions that are done on each visit, such as attending a local community crafts fair or homecoming football game.

❀ Brighten the home of distant friends or relatives, and remind them of you by sending flowers for each season, like a pot of tulips in the spring, a basket of daisies in the summer, a mum in the fall, and a poinsettia in the winter.

❀ While visiting a relative who can't get out, stock the shelves with everyday items such as coffee, toiletries, paper plates, candy.

❀ Pitch in and help with heavy yard work or house maintenance for an older relative during your visit.

❀ Plan to eat out frequently when you visit or pick up items from the deli, so you will not be placing a burden for meals on your host. Or offer to cook dinner for your host.

❀ Take a tape recorder, and record memories while an older relative reminisces about the past.

❀ Take pictures during your visit. Arrange them in an album, and send it to your friend so that he or she can enjoy the visit all over again.

❀ To help someone through the transition of leaving home, write frequently the first several months about what's happening at home.

❀ For college students, fill a small album of photos of their childhood and pictures of their neighborhood, schools, and family to take with them.

❀ Purchase either phone gift certificates or calling cards that anyone can use to call home. Wrap the phone cards up with a copy of the *E.T.* video.

❀ Encourage two-way correspondence by sending a self-addressed, stamped envelope.

❀ Get a long-distance friend an e-mail address so she or he can communicate as often as necessary with family and friends.

❀ If special occasions will be missed, have everyone sign a card, and also include a photo of the event to send to the person who couldn't be there.

❀ In your correspondence, send clippings from magazines and local newspapers that you know would interest a long-distance friend.

❀ Have a prearranged time set for a phone date, so that everyone can look forward to talking person-to-person.

CHAPTER FIVE

Work

Most of our time is taken up with our work. Sometimes, finding the position that is right for you can be extremely difficult and can sometimes take years. Most people go through several careers before finding the one that is a perfect fit. Though many of us find ourselves at one time or another in a job that we dislike, we usually find a way to make our work meaningful. Our jobs become a central way of contributing to society, so making sure that we go about our work in a caring and respectful way is important.

Not only should we try to care about our work, we should take care of ourselves and our co-workers at work. With respectful caring for one another, the workplace can be a safe and friendly environment that helps each of us to do our best. The following chapter provides ways for you, your family, and your co-workers to support one another through the demands of work.

Look around you, first in your own family, then among your friends and neighbors, and see whether there be not someone whose little burden you can lighten, whose little cares you may lessen, whose little pleasures you can promote, whose little wants and wishes you can gratify.

LITTLE THINGS

Searching for a New Job

Scott had worked for this company twenty-six years, starting his career the day after he graduated from college. He put his work first, often forfeiting events with his family. He knew the company was having some financial trouble, and he did his part to motivate the people who worked for him to work harder.

When his supervisor told him he was being laid off with one month's severance pay, Scott was sure there had been a mistake. Meetings with his superiors only reiterated what his direct supervisor had told him. It was clear that their decision was firm; his job was eliminated.

Scott didn't know how to go home and tell his family what had happened, mostly because he had not accepted it himself. He had been fortunate enough to give his family a comfortable life. His son would be attending college in two years, and Scott had promised to pay his tuition for the out-of-state college he chose.

Many companies in the area had gone through a similar downsizing. Scott discovered finding similar employment was not going to be easy. He spent hours each day sending out résumés and following up on leads, only to find that he was competing with many others for the few jobs there were.

After six months of job hunting with no success, a discouraged Scott sat down with his family, and together they realized they were going to have to make some major changes. Scott decided to take a job managing a fast-food restaurant. The compensation was not as much as the salary he had been used to, and the shift he worked didn't allow him much time with his family. His wife, Mary, went back to work as a substitute teacher. Scott and Mary told their two sons they were going to have to give up some of their afternoon school activities to get part-time jobs and help save money for college. Also, they asked their sons to consider going to the local community college.

At a time when they had expected to feel comfortable and secure, they felt anything but. Everything had changed, and although they tried to make the most of the changes, they found themselves wistfully thinking about how secure life had been just a year earlier.

* If someone is unemployed, encourage her or him to start or maintain a good physical fitness routine. Even a daily vigorous walk can help reduce stress and tension.
* Encourage the unemployed to use their talents in other productive ways. This is the ideal time to get involved with a charity, church, or community event where they can help others.
* At holidays, give the family a gift of entertainment tickets, like movie passes and pizza gift certificates.
* If the unemployed person needs to update computer

skills, offer to loan the use of your system and any tutorials or self-help manuals you might have.

❀ Discuss what kind of employment your friend is seeking and offer your assistance in preparing résumés or contacting employers. Offer to type a letter of recommendation. Purchase stamps, stationery, and matching envelopes for sending out résumés.

❀ If the person has a particular hobby, such as sewing or woodworking, purchase some new supplies to keep him or her busy.

❀ Give the person a certificate for a massage during this stressful time.

❀ If the person is seeking employment in a new field or is thinking about going back to college, help by providing a trade catalog or a list of classes.

❀ When the person has found a new job, celebrate by throwing a party for him or her with balloons, lots of friends, and family. Bring work-related gifts, like a new briefcase.

❀ When someone begins a new job, send flowers on the first day, or make plans to take the person to lunch.

❀ Purchase a copy of *What Color Is Your Parachute?,* by Richard Nelson Bolles, for someone going through a career change.

Caring for Anyone Having a Bad Day

Having all experienced bad days, we know that on such days we often just feel like being left alone. But a kind gesture from a co-worker or a friend can help you break through your bad mood. Do your best to help someone who's having a rough day and let them know you are there for them if they need it:

❀ Keep encouragement cards handy for when you see someone having "one of those days." Sign one and place in a spot where the person will be sure to see it.

❀ For someone having a bad day, offer a tissue, a smile, and these words: "Go ahead and cry if you need to."

❀ If you notice a co-worker having a bad day, give the person a five-minute break: take your co-worker to the vending machine and buy something he or she chooses. Sometimes just walking away from the problem for a few minutes alleviates the difficulty of the situation.

❀ Simply ask, "How can I help?"

❀ Acknowledge out loud that someone is having a bad day. A sympathetic ear provides tremendous relief.

❀ When you see someone is having a bad day, walk to a nearby office and call the person, just to listen to her or his problems.

❀ Find some humor in the situation. There usually is something funny in every problem.

❀ Almost anything you do for someone will lighten the

load. If you are eating a bagel, offer the person half. Say, "I see you need this more than I do."

❁ Put words of encouragement on a yellow sticky note, and attach it to their computer.

❁ Go out and buy the person a lottery ticket, allowing them to dream momentarily how their life might change if they won.

❁ Leave a copy of the newspaper comic section for them to read.

❁ Have a "bad day" trophy, which gets moved around the office to whomever is having a bad day.

❁ If you are having a bad day, put a warning sign on your door or desk that advises everybody to approach with caution.

❁ Call and send a sing-a-gram.

Commuting Is Harder Than You Think

Katherine was excited about being called to interview for a teaching job she had recently applied for. She had been in her current professor position about eight years now and felt it was time to move on. When she saw the ad in the newspaper for a department head with a university located farther west, she wasn't sure whether or not to apply, given that it was about 120 miles from where they lived. It was hard for her to think about giving up her current position; she had developed a fierce loyalty to the school and enjoyed the faculty members and students. She had sent out her résumé, never really thinking she would be contacted. Now here she was, preparing for the interview, realizing that she had a fairly good chance of getting the position.

She and her husband, Roy, had talked about what might happen if Katherine got the job. Roy was established in his career as the overall divisional manager at the bank, overseeing twelve branches. He had worked hard to obtain that position and was content with his status. Their three children attended various schools, two in high school and one in middle school. They all struggled with Katherine's interviewing for a position so far away, not really wanting to relocate, given the children's desire to stay in their current schools until they graduated, along with Roy's preference to keep his current job.

Katherine had a clearer understanding of the job responsibilities after her interview. She knew she really wanted this job. This position offered a lot more in terms of salary, benefits, and the university's prestige. When the interview ended, she was told she was their number one candidate for the position and that they would be contacting her in the near future.

As she drove home, she felt torn between her own excitement and concern about the reaction from her family. The family sat down that night and talked it through. Katherine decided that if she was offered the position, she would accept it. She had already concluded that she would make the drive each day rather than asking her family to move.

The following Monday the phone rang, and Katherine was offered the position. A month later, she began her daily commute of 120 miles each way to her new job. At first it was easy; the newness of the job kept her spirits high during the drive. She found herself using the time in the car to think about how to make positive changes in her department. Eventually the drive became tedious. Katherine never realized how fatiguing three to four hours in the car were each day. She missed family events such as eating breakfast together, attending school activities, and gathering for dinner. Sometimes Katherine questioned whether she had made the right decision, and she felt torn between her career and family.

❀ Purchase a cellular phone for emergencies and to stay in touch while the commuter is en route.

- Get books on tape from the library, and offer to return them.
- Purchase cassettes or CDs for the commuter's car.
- If the person is interested in a foreign language or some other topic, get a tape on that issue.
- As a family, support the family member who is commuting by giving them some time to unwind from the weather, traffic, and the long hours when they return home.
- Leave inspirational messages in the commuter's car, such as a simple, "We're thinking of you" or "We miss you, hurry home."
- Purchase a small recorder that the person could use as a journal or to record memos of what needs to be done upon arriving at home or work.
- Buy a neck pillow that works well in a car.
- Fill a small basket with snacks such as juice, pretzels, peanuts, and crackers.
- Give the commuter a thermos with a flip-top pour spout so she or he can easily pour beverages while driving.
- Purchase a frame with double-sided tape for attaching a family photo to the dashboard.
- Offer to help with maintenance items such as yard work or house maintenance so that family members can make the most of their time together.

Caring for Someone Traveling

Many people think business travel is glamorous, but ask anyone who travels frequently and she or he will tell you that being away from family and friends often can be extremely stressful and lonely. Letting those who are away from home know that you are thinking about them can help make their trip more manageable. Here are some ideas for showing that the traveler is in your thoughts:

❀ Slip a card or letter in their suitcase, which they will find when they reach their destination.

❀ For someone staying at a hotel, call ahead and arrange for flowers or a gift certificate for a restaurant.

❀ Send a card that will be there when your loved one arrives.

❀ Pack stationery for the traveler as well as stamps, so she or he can keep in touch during an extended stay.

❀ Go to the airport to see your friend off, and be there when he or she returns. Make "Welcome Home" signs to hold at the gate.

❀ Pack snacks such as bagels, raisins, and nuts.

❀ Give the latest best-seller in paperback for reading on the plane.

❀ Lend a portable CD player and CDs for traveling. This is great for waiting areas in airports or train stations. Also, it can be used later in the hotel or outdoors for relaxation.

- For someone who travels frequently, purchase a suitcase with wheels and a long handle.
- Call ahead to the hotel and determine if there is a fitness facility. Encourage your traveler to take appropriate clothes and use the gym as a stress release from traveling.
- Give a neck pillow for traveling by car, plane, or train.
- Give your friend a small cassette player with books on tape from the library.
- Give your loved one a calling card so she or he can call you easily en route.
- Borrow or purchase a portable VCR for long car trips.
- Loan someone a cellular phone for a trip.
- Call ahead to the hotel and have breakfast sent to the traveler's room, along with the morning paper.
- Give travelers visitor information relative to their destination. Check into special events such as plays and sports events they may want to attend.
- Get the fax number at the hotel and send messages. Have children draw pictures to fax.
- Pack bottled water for a traveler to help avoid dehydration.

Was Taking This Job the Right Thing to Do?

Ed and Melinda were feeling great about their lives. They both had successful careers and lived in a small community in a home they had built on a picturesque river. Their life revolved around their only son, Tom, nine, who completed their happiness.

Ed worked for a company that was increasing its global market. He was the most senior manager in the local division of the company, and to further his career, he needed to take an overseas assignment. Ed and Melinda had struggled with the decision each time Ed was offered a promotion. He had turned down the last several opportunities.

The company asked Ed to take a three-month assignment in Europe to help one of their operations, and this time Ed said yes. The family had never been separated before, so they awaited Ed's departure with trepidation. Ed and Tom, who had such a close relationship, seemed to suffer the most. It was hard to tell who had more tears in their eyes when Melinda and Tom drove Ed to the airport. Ed couldn't seem to find the right words to explain to Tom why he would be gone so long. And while he was away, Ed felt despondent every time he called, for Tom pleaded with him to come home. Was this next promotion really worth this?

❋ For those on an extended assignment, offer to videotape

key events of their children and mail it to them.

- To alleviate the loneliness of being away from home, suggest that family members, friends, and relatives write a chain letter weekly to keep their loved one updated on daily activities.

- Help small children understand when someone will return by marking off the days on a calendar.

- Give the person leaving a small album of recent pictures that have been taken of the whole family.

- Send appropriate seasonal memories while the loved one is away—an envelope of fall leaves or pressed spring flowers to remind them of home.

- Pack some of their favorite items to enjoy while they're away, such as individualized packages of coffee or tea or their favorite chocolates.

- Inquire about being added as a guest to their work voicemail box, then leave personal messages often from the whole family.

- While someone is away, clip interesting articles from the local newspaper and send them.

- Help the parent at home by offering to drive their children to and from activities.

- Mail a packet weekly of artwork or school assignments that the children have done.

Caring for Busy Parents

With kids there are always so many details and so little time. Finding minutes in the day to get everything done that needs to be done seems like an impossible task. With so much to take care of, we need to feel that others are looking out for us as well. Here are some ways for parents to support each other and themselves, as well as ways you can support a loved one who is a busy parent:

❁ Help set up child-care options for snow days, sick days, and holidays. Keep on hand a list of neighbors, relatives, and trusted friends who can be called at the last minute to take the children.

❁ Pick up parenting magazines for parents to browse. There are dozens on the newsstands, and most all contain information on raising your children and how to balance work and family issues.

❁ Make a date twice a month to go out as a couple. Book ahead with a trusted sitter. Use one evening to catch up on how the kids are doing, and one just to reconnect as a couple.

❁ To beat the "just home from work and day care with dinner to be made" transition time, have a local high school student come over several afternoons to play with the kids while dinner is being prepared.

❁ Offer to run errands for working parents, like going to the post office or drugstore or picking up dry cleaning.

* When errands have to be done after a long day at the office and at day care, try to make a game out of doing them together. If possible, grab a snack together first.

* When deciding on extracurricular events that your children want to be involved with, check with other friends or neighbors for their children's interests so that you could arrange for carpooling.

* Stock your car with juice boxes, pretzels, raisins, and crackers to offer on the way to and from day care, especially if you have a long drive.

* Designate a spot in your house, such as the hallway by the outside door, where everything that needs to go to school, work, or day care is placed. Give each child a backpack or duffel bag for their items.

* Give yourself a break and your child a special lunch treat by picking up pre-made lunch items from the grocery store. Pack them in lunchboxes on hectic mornings when you're having to get everyone out extra early because you have a meeting.

* Involve your children at an early age in helping to pack items they need for school or day care.

More Caring for Busy Parents

Because busy parents need all the help they can get, here are even more ways to support the busiest people you know:

❀ Have a magnetic or erasable wall calendar where all family events, school notes, reminders, errands, and chores can be put for everyone to see. List names of those responsible for each.

❀ As you look ahead in your business calendar, mark off time for your children. Pencil them in for a lunch date with you or for breakfast before school, or plan a half-day vacation to attend a field trip with them.

❀ Make it easy to keep up with memories. Have disposable cameras around the house to take those "too cute" shots. Keep the video camera's battery charged. Have a large tub with a lid for each child to keep treasured items such as a school program, report card, favorite pair of tennis shoes they have outgrown, and so forth.

❀ Decide on the required household chores, and divide equally among the family. If possible, hire out the main housecleaning, but have the rest of the items on a list and plan a specific time each week when they must be accomplished, like Thursday night, to allow for "fun" time on the weekend.

❀ Use a family planning calendar to note what the family may want to do weekends in advance, even if everyone wants a do-nothing, kick-back kind of weekend.

❀ Find exercise routines the whole family can be involved with. Join an athletic club or YMCA where everyone can use the facilities. Get the family outside bike riding or roller-blading. Even young children can come along in an appropriate backpack or stroller.

❀ Keep sing-a-long cassettes, crayons, and coloring books in the car for those times when you're stuck in traffic.

❀ Organize a baby-sitting co-op with other working parents you know from work, day care, or your neighborhood. While one set of parents can enjoy time to themselves, the children can play with friends.

❀ Have emergency quick-fix dinners on hand for those nights when you get home late and everyone is crabby. Open a prepared frozen entrée or a box of macaroni and cheese.

❀ Plan one night a week that everyone is home. Plan games and have everyone help prepare the meal.

Finding Life After Retirement

The retirement party was a lavish event. There was plenty of time for reminiscing about the thirty-eight years Al had been with the company. The evening ended with Al's successor, Pete, giving a poignant speech on Al's contributions to the company and how much he would be missed. The guests applauded and held their glasses for a final toast. Al and Joyce held hands, looking at each other, not needing any words to communicate.

The first week at home was wonderful. Al kept congratulating himself on his decision to retire, wondering why he had waited so long. Joyce was still working as a teacher, so she was gone during the day. He kept busy with golf and little projects that had piled up for years. However, he found it almost disturbingly quiet without the hustle and bustle of problems, questions, and constant communication he was used to at work. Some days he couldn't find anyone who had free time for golf. But in a few weeks, he knew that Joyce would be on summer break and they could have an all-summer vacation.

Joyce sensed his frustration when she returned home from work every night. She usually found the house in disarray, with Al's different projects started but never quite finished. During the two weeks before Joyce's summer off, they both seemed tense as they adjusted to their new roles.

The first week of summer vacation, Joyce and Al went to

their cottage. They kept their usual routine of visiting with neighbors, boating, and window-shopping in the quaint lakeside village. When the week ended and Sunday evening came, they weren't sure what to do. They didn't have any reason to go back home, so they decided to stay at their cottage.

Al was having a very difficult time adjusting from being someone previously "in charge" to having no demands on him. He sat by the phone each day, wishing someone would call for his advice. The phone didn't ring, the company had simply moved on.

By the end of the summer, Joyce was ready for school to start. She watched Al wandering around each day without any plans. She felt his growing bitterness being transferred to her.

She decided to check on potential part-time job opportunities that would fit Al's skills, someone looking for retirees with good business skills and years of practical, hands-on experience. The last weekend at the lake, she suggested they go out for dinner. She told him she sensed he was unhappy and wanted to help him to find a way to fulfill his life again. She shared the information about part-time opportunities with him. Much to Joyce's surprise, Al was moved to tears because Joyce had known exactly what he needed.

The next week, Joyce went back to school and Al began life as a consultant. He found it even more rewarding than his previous job, because of the variety of assignments with challenging problems. The hours were perfect for his new lifestyle.

❀ Provide a list of community volunteer needs, such as helping with United Way or food banks, where retired people's skills could be used and appreciated.

❀ Suggest a membership at a local health club so they can begin an exercise routine.

❀ Plan a weekly evening of cards or games with other friends.

❀ Suggest they spend time with their grandchildren or someone else's and teach them skills such as fixing a car or making something out of wood.

❀ If you have young grandchildren, consider baby-sitting for them one morning a week to stay connected.

❀ Suggest they record their life for their children and grandchildren. A book to help get started is *For Our Children's Children*. Recordings can be in writing or on tape so they will hear a voice.

❀ Write letters to your children telling them how much they mean to you. These will be cherished forever. For examples, pick up the book *Letters for Our Children*; it is a collection of wisdom from ordinary people who want to pass their life's lessons on to their children.

❀ If you are retired and your spouse is still working, pick your spouse up for lunch once a week. Use this opportunity to discuss how things are working out for both of you.

❀ Recommend a health club to use this extra time to

really concentrate on their health. Suggest taking preventative measures, such as quitting smoking, losing weight, and developing a daily regimen of exercising.

- ❀ Contact a local college to inquire whether they use retired business people as guest speakers.

- ❀ Suggest to the retiree that he or she and spouse take a cooking class together.

- ❀ Give tickets to a travelogue presentation which could inspire curiosity about new cities and other interesting travel.

- ❀ Suggest lunch or coffee once a month or on a regular basis.

- ❀ Check into financial planning seminars which are held locally.

- ❀ Find out if there are retirement support groups available.

Caring for Co-workers

Our co-workers are the people we spend the most time with each day, so it is important that we support one another and feel like a team. We all have been helped through busy times with the help of a caring co-worker. Make sure you notice and acknowledge the support you get at work. Here are some ways for you and your co-workers to recognize one another:

❈ Put together a list of all co-workers' birthdays, then have each person bring a cake or other dessert for the person's birthday following their own. This allows everyone to participate, and no one is burdened with organizing all of the birthdays. Make sure to gather everyone around to sing "Happy Birthday" and share in the dessert together.

❈ Several times a year, get the whole crew together and go out for lunch. Pick an unusual restaurant, which can be a conversation starter for a large group of people.

❈ Bring in doughnuts, muffins, or bagels some morning for the whole department, just to get everyone's morning jump-started.

❈ When someone in your department is getting married or expecting a new baby, take up a collection and present it in a card. Cash is always appreciated so they can purchase what is really needed.

❈ Acknowledge your co-workers daily by a cheery "good

morning," or "hello," really looking into their eyes when you see them. "Have a nice day," when sincerely expressed, is never lost on anyone.

❁ Say "thank you," even for the simplest task of someone bringing you some supplies you requested or for returning your phone call.

❁ When you see your co-worker is having a tough day, possibly feeling the pressure of a big meeting, offer your support in any way possible. Offer to help make copies, set up audio-visual equipment, or bring them whatever they need while preparing.

❁ Show respect and courtesy for all your co-workers, regardless of their position within the company.

❁ Try to consider what tasks you give others that you could do for yourself. Rather than asking the assistant to dial someone's number for you, ask her or him to prepare a phone index for you, and dial the phone yourself.

❁ If your co-worker receives a promotion, acknowledge this with a note, a lunch out, or even flowers.

❁ Get your co-workers together to plan a holiday party outside of the office.

Caring at Work

Here are some more ways to give and receive support at work:

❀ At holiday times, ask co-workers to get involved in helping a charity, such as collecting food for the local food bank, participating in a bowl-a-thon, or spending a few hours at the blood bank. The act of coming together to support someone less fortunate is more meaningful than giving gifts to one another.

❀ Consider keeping the community spirit going all year long. After the holidays, organize your co-workers to put on a fundraiser or to participate in one that is already planned. The local volunteer center can help you find an organization that will fit your resources.

❀ Develop your own trademark by leaving the same gift on someone's desk, like an apple or a small bag of candy.

❀ Encourage humor and laughter in the workplace. Post copies of cartoons that are not offensive and that everyone would relate to.

❀ Consider starting a group fund where a collection is taken periodically to send flowers to co-workers who lose family members or who become ill.

❀ When you go to the fax machine to pick up your fax, take the time to sort out the ones going to others, and deliver them to their desks.

❀ When you anticipate a company meeting might have

some tense moments, bring in a big bag of lollipops, and pass them around the room to break the tension and possibly even bring out a smile or two.

❀ Celebrate the holidays together by having a potluck lunch. Ask everyone to sign up to bring something.

❀ Bring a pot of coffee around in the morning, and serve your co-workers.

❀ Donate some of your vacation time for a co-worker who must take time off work due to a severe health condition.

❀ Put a "Welcome Back" banner over a co-worker's desk when she or he is returning from a business trip or vacation.

❀ Acknowledge a co-worker's "work anniversary" or major milestones in his or her career. Bring flowers or take the person out to lunch.

❀ For a new employee, provide bagels and fresh fruit for her or his desk, thereby encouraging others to introduce themselves.

❀ Plan a luncheon for a co-worker who is leaving. Offer to write a letter of recommendation for her or him.

❀ Share a copy of *The Seven Habits of Highly Effective People,* by Steven Covey with a friend at work.

CHAPTER SIX

Caring for Yourself

Those of us who have discovered the social benefits of volunteerism and caring for others may find ourselves feeling guilty about taking time just for ourselves. But the simple fact is that we can't take care of those around us unless we take care of ourselves. You need care just as much as your family and friends do. You know what you need better than anyone else does, and you are the best person to give yourself the personal attention you need. Through self-care, you give yourself the strength to keep doing caring things in the world. We have collected here many ideas for how to spend the time that you set aside just for you.

Caring Ways to Spend Your Family Time

Weekends are often busy with errands and duties, so by Sunday the opportunity to enjoy yourself has faded. Try these ideas to plan for a weekend of fun. Holiday weekends are not the only time for family relaxation:

❀ In the middle of a northern winter, plan a beach party. Have everyone wear shorts and T-shirts. Serve hot dogs, potato salad, and ice cream sundaes. Play Beach Boys songs. For games, do the limbo.

❀ Designate one night a month as game night. Get out board games, checkers, and dominoes. Invite friends.

❀ Have friends plan a progressive dinner once a month where everyone is responsible for part of the meal. The hors d'oeurvres are at one house, the salad at another, the main course at someone else's, and dessert and coffee at another's. Rotate which course you are responsible for each month.

❀ Find others who enjoy the same hobby as you. If you like quilting or woodworking, arrange for your friends to meet regularly to talk about and/or perform the hobby. If you love antiques, find friends who will attend antique shows with you.

❀ Explore local attractions that are new to you. Call for tickets to a play, or visit the museum in your city.

❀ Experiment with a new recipe once a week. Have a

different family member find the recipe and prepare the meal. The rest of the family could rate the meal with cards showing numbers 1 through 10, like in the Olympics.

❀ Invite family members over, and videotape or use a cassette to ask them about their childhood. Have each family member tell about their most important memories as well as their recollections of you.

❀ Have a party where all bring their unorganized photos and empty albums and spend the evening organizing their photos. Afterward everyone will be able to share their finished albums with one another.

❀ Ask children what they would like to learn, then make time to teach them cooking, fishing, or using a video camera.

❀ On a warm summer day, take a blanket outside and lie down to watch the clouds for a few hours. Children love this one.

❀ Let kids plan a slumber party. Help them send invitations, plan the activities, and prepare the food.

❀ Plan a night at a local hotel for the family every couple of months. Take games and swimsuits, and plan to relax together.

❀ Have a room or basement for teenagers where you have a Ping-Pong table, a pool table, or a card table for games and cards.

- Try ethnic recipes at home, or visit a local restaurant.

- Have a costume or theme party on a non-holiday. Have everyone dress up as *Star Wars* or Disney characters.

- Make everyday or weekend meals special by using "good" china and lighting candles.

- Plan a party around the theme of a favorite movie or actor. For example, show Tom Cruise movies.

- Plan a few hours to visit a neighboring town and take in the sights.

- Children, as well as seniors, like the activity of people-watching. So plan a visit to a local airport, mall, or train station.

- Have the whole family participate in fundraising walks.

- Plan a weekend to plant flowers or maintain a garden. Even if you don't have a yard, you can rent space to have your own garden.

- During holiday times and summer months, plan social activities the whole family will enjoy.

- Try to arrange a one-week vacation each year as a family.

Caring for Yourself

We've spent this whole book thinking about how to take care of others. Now it's time to think about yourself. Many people forget to take as much time for themselves as they need. Pamper yourself when you want to. You deserve it:

❀ Take a meditation or yoga class, and learn the art of relaxation. Then practice it daily.

❀ Spend a few minutes each day doing one thing that makes you feel peaceful, such as enjoying a burning candle, a cup of coffee, or a good book.

❀ While most of us spend our time with other people from the minute we wake up, it is good to have solitude. Find an activity that you enjoy and then do it alone, such as going to a movie, having lunch in a restaurant, exercising, or shopping.

❀ Purchase a journal for yourself that matches your writing needs. Make sure to get paper with the texture you like to write on and a cover that invites you to pick it up. Once you have a journal, write in it several times a week. Express your hopes, dreams, fears, and your feelings today.

❀ Pay attention to your daydreams. The ones you have repeatedly may provide you with information about what you really want out of life. Read *Using Your Dreams to Unlock Your Creativity,* by Veronica Tonay, Ph.D.

- ❀ Wear the clothes and hair style that *you* want. Plan activities that make you happy.
- ❀ Help others. Volunteer at a church or organization that gives you self-satisfaction.
- ❀ Read inspirational books such as *Soulwork* and *A Soulworker's Companion,* both by BettyClare Moffatt. These books show you how to open your heart and soul.
- ❀ Feel good about yourself by taking care of yourself. Vow that you'll pay attention to the right things to eat, and develop a consistent exercise routine that will work for your schedule.
- ❀ Smile all the time. Even when things aren't going your way, reach inside and offer a smile to those you meet. It will make you feel better.
- ❀ Set your alarm early, and have some time to yourself to read, reflect, organize, or just enjoy that morning beverage in peace.
- ❀ Take a few minutes at the end of the day to stand outside and look at the stars and moon.
- ❀ Find time each day to watch a favorite TV show, like an old rerun of *I Love Lucy* or part of your favorite movie.

More Caring for Yourself

And because you can never spoil yourself too much, here are even more ways to be good to you:

❀ Take a leisurely trip through a bookstore. Select some books you'd like to browse, then relax and read over coffee in their café.

❀ Renew yourself by changing something in your personal style: your haircut, your skirt length or belt width, a favorite color in blazer or blouse.

❀ Lock the bathroom door and indulge in a bath. Have your favorite drink, book, and music close by.

❀ Sign up for that class you've been thinking about.

❀ Call someone special, for no reason, just because a conversation with that person always makes you feel good.

❀ Change the monotony of your meals by using candles during the middle of the week.

❀ Immerse yourself in a hobby you enjoy but rarely take the time to do: bake a loaf of bread from scratch, make homemade pie, get out your watercolors, or spend time in your garden.

❀ Once a month, stop the clock in your crazy, hectic life by making time stand still. Plan no activities for the day. Stay in your bathrobe all day if you feel like it.

❀ Pick some fresh flowers and put them in a bowl of water. Take time to enjoy the serenity of them as they float ever so peacefully, releasing their fragrance.

* Get a pair of extra soft pajamas, the kind that give you a hug.

* Establish a weekly ritual of doing something just for you. For example, go out for breakfast by yourself every Tuesday morning. Pick up your favorite newspaper on the way. Read, relax, and collect your thoughts, all while being waited on.

* Step back in time by playing board games with children. It will provide a few laughs and smiles, and most importantly will endear you to the children who appreciated your taking the time to play with them.

* Have something special in the house that's just for you, with no obligation to share it. Stash away those little candy bars that you crave or a special jar of marmalade for your toast.

* Decide to expand your mind and learn something new. Pick up a book that's out of your normal genre, visit a museum you've never been to, go to a sporting event that you've never attended.

* Buy yourself a holiday gift. Who else knows what you *really* want?

* Take the time to develop and keep a best-friend relationship.

About the Authors

Beth Hubbard Kitzinger is a manager at a large automotive company. She has a business administration degree from Michigan State University, an engineering degree from Lansing College, and a Master's degree in engineering management.

She is the mother of two boys, and she enjoys freelance writing for magazines.

Linda Davies Rockey has held a variety of positions from legal secretary to claims analyst.

Diagnosed with Crohn's disease at age eighteen, Linda has spent her adult years counseling and supporting others with Crohn's disease. She is the President of the Crohn's and Colitis Foundation of America—Lansing Satellite. Linda is the mother of a teenage daughter.

Linda and **Beth** have been close friends for almost twenty years. Knowing how much their friendship and support has meant to each other is what inspired them to write this book.